more than just a
name

preserving

our
Baptist
identity

R. STANTON NORMAN

BROADMAN
& HOLMAN
PUBLISHERS

Nashville, Tennessee

0–8054–2020–7

Published by Broadman & Holman Publishers,
Nashville, Tennessee

Dewey Decimal Classification: 230
Subject Heading: BAPTIST DOCTRINE

Library of Congress Cataloging-in-Publication Data

Norman, R. Stanton, 1963–
    More than just a name : preserving our Baptist identity /
R. Stanton Norman.
        p. cm.
Includes bibliographical references.
ISBN 0–8054–2020–7 (pb.)
1. Baptists—Doctrines. I. Title.

BX6331.2 .N67 2001
230'.6—dc21
                                                          2001025534

1 2 3 4 5 6 7 8 9 10 05 04 03 02 01

Contents

Foreword

As the twenty-first century dawns, Baptists face an identity crisis that threatens our continued vitality and faithfulness in work and witness. This identity crisis was not, in the main, brought on by events or pressures from without the denomination. No, we have brought this crisis on ourselves.

For too many years, Baptists in general, and Southern Baptists in particular, have allowed theological and doctrinal neglect to erode the very foundation of our identity. At first, these doctrines were simply taken for granted. They faced no direct denial or confrontation. Lulled into a season of theological self-confidence, Baptists of the last century directed their energies and attention into ambitious programs and numerical growth. They were confident that the doctrinal foundation was safe, secure, and sacred to all Baptists. They were wrong.

In the next stage, many Baptists became convinced that doctrines were really not all that important. Activism had replaced doctrinal teaching and attention, and the attacks on cherished doctrines seemed safely limited to the periphery of denominational life. Other denominations were embroiled in theological controversies, but Southern Baptists wanted nothing of that.

Nevertheless, as continued doctrinal compromises became glaringly apparent, and as direct attacks on cherished Baptist doctrines became more common, voices of concern were raised. At some point, a critical mass of concern and alarm prompted an attempt to reclaim and reassert the great doctrinal heritage that gave birth to the Baptist movement, and is the foundation for Baptist witness.

The controversy that has shaped the Southern Baptist Convention over the past thirty years comes down to a great struggle to define Baptist identity. Denominational controversies, like family conflicts, are often heated and difficult to understand. Often, only after the dust clears are the issues seen in clear light.

In this book, Stan Norman grapples with the most important issues facing Baptists today. He is a theologian, and he writes with a theologian's insight and care. Nevertheless, he is also a committed Southern Baptist, and he writes with evident love and deep concern for his beloved denomination.

He asks, "What makes a Baptist a Baptist?" And that question is at the center of the search for Baptist identity. Of course, there is no individual Baptist without a Baptist congregation. Staunch advocates of believers' church, Baptists must answer this question of identity together, as well as individually. Eventually, the answer to this question will shape our churches, our denomination, and every aspect of our work together.

Theological recovery will not come without a price, and that price is first paid in the hard work of sorting out the issues and facing the options with honesty. Years of doctrinal apathy and neglect must be reversed by the present generation. The hard work of recovery will demand our best thinking, our most honest reflection, and an absolute commitment to honoring God's truth and the faith once for all delivered to the saints.

Stan Norman offers keen insights as Southern Baptists face this task. He asks the hard questions and guides modern Baptists through the richness of the Baptist tradition in reconstructing our doctrinal heritage.

Dr. Norman seeks to define Baptist distinctives—not in an exercise of denominational hubris, but in an effort to recover what it means for Baptists to be Baptists. In a helpful way, he clears the fog from many of the most vexing issues and offers insights from our heritage. For this, we are all in his debt.

Critical issues such as confessionalism, biblical authority, soul competency, religious experience, and congregationalism are confronted with candor, and investigated with care. Individual readers may disagree with portions of Dr. Norman's analysis, and some of his proposals, but every reader will be enriched by working through these issues.

The urgency of this task cannot be ignored. In this generation, Baptists will either recover our denominational heritage and rebuild our doctrinal foundations, or in the next generation there will be no authentic Baptist witness. Danger signs unmistakably mark the horizon.

We are reaping the harvest of doctrinal neglect. Among many of our people, the most basic doctrinal issues are unknown and unconfronted. Pragmatism and experientialism have so shaped the modern Baptist mind that many have lost even the ability to think theologically.

The current generation of Baptist young people knows little about Baptist doctrine, and is searching for some solid ground on which they can base their lives and Christian discipleship. With the Bible as our authority, we must relearn the basics, and reclaim the richness of our doctrinal heritage.

We must rediscover a lost and neglected wisdom, and reconstruct the foundation and framework of our faith. It is high time we get about this task.

R. Albert Mohler, Jr.
President
The Southern Baptist Theological Seminary

Introduction:
Distinctively Baptist?

....

I am a Baptist. I was born into a Baptist family and was raised in Baptist churches. Denominationally, I am a Southern Baptist. I am proud of my Baptist heritage and of my denominational affiliation. I love Baptists and have given my life in part to assist them in their pursuit of God's will and the extension of his kingdom.

BACKGROUND OF THIS STUDY:
A PERSONAL PILGRIMAGE

In spite of my love for my Baptist heritage, I was an adult and a student at Southwestern Baptist Theological Seminary before I began to seriously wonder, *Why am I a Baptist?* Other than my upbringing, what reasons did I have for being a

Baptist? Furthermore, what does it really mean to be a Baptist? As I reflected on these questions, others began to surface. For example, are Baptists really that different from other Christians? If so, how?

Over the course of the next few years, these and other concerns continued to haunt me. I was, in a sense, suffering from a theological-denominational identity crisis. In addition to this, my life's situation further aggravated my internal conflict. I was serving as a pastor of a Southern Baptist church. I was receiving ministerial training at a Baptist institution of graduate studies. Yet, being a pastor of a Baptist church and a student at a Baptist school did not provide the immediate answers I longed to have. To make matters worse, my own denomination, the Southern Baptist Convention, was engulfed within a conflict that could be described in part as a search for its own Baptist identity. The conflict of the SBC to define its theological identity mirrored my own struggle. All realms of my professional and denominational life seemed consumed with the question of Baptist identity. I finally determined to embark upon a pilgrimage to discover exactly what makes a Baptist a Baptist. This study is in large measure the fruit of that search.

A SIMPLE QUESTION?

"What makes a Baptist a Baptist?" This question sounds so simple that any moderately informed person should be able to answer it. Yet, the seeming simplicity of this question disguises how difficult it is to answer. Questions like these often mask complex issues, and this one is no different. Ask any Baptist, "What makes a Baptist a Baptist?" and you may receive as many answers as there are Baptists. Baptists typically agree that they have a distinctive theological identity. They disagree, however, on the definition of this identity.

Baptists frequently forge their distinctive identity in the fires of controversy. More often than not, non-Baptists have often forced Baptists to defend their unique theological perspectives. For example, in early colonial America, Baptists struggled to practice their faith according to their convictions against the governing authorities and other Christian denominations. Baptists often refused to pay taxes that went to support the state-established churches, especially in colonial New England and Virginia. In many cases, they refused to have their children baptized as infants into state-sanctioned or state-sponsored churches. The governments of various colonial charters persecuted Baptists economically, socially, and politically. On rare occasions some Baptists were even beaten for practicing their convictions. Despite these harsh conditions, Baptists not only continued to develop and articulate their distinctive theological identity, but they also challenged other Christian denominations to justify their own doctrinal positions. Baptists have never been people to "run from a good fight" or "compromise their convictions," even in the harshest of conditions.

Not only have Baptists been pressed from without to define their distinctive identity; they have also argued with one another on the question of "what makes a Baptist a Baptist." Many opinions have been offered on what constitutes true Baptist distinctives. Some emphasize doctrines like the priesthood of all believers, believer's baptism, a regenerate church membership, the primacy of the Scriptures for faith and practice, or congregational autonomy. Others point to ideas such as religious freedom, soul competency, or the lordship of Christ as the defining criteria. One popular answer often heard in Baptist pulpits is that Baptists believe in "the Book, the blood, and the blessed hope." Baptists are hard-pressed to give a definitive answer that represents all Baptists.

Another approach commonly found in the quest to identify Baptist distinctives is "appealing to the Baptist precedent." This is the practice of using statements like "Baptists have always believed this" or "this [particular doctrine] has always been a part of the distinctive Baptist identity." These appeals are often cited as the undisputed truth that definitively answers the question and brings immediate resolution to the debate. This practice is found both in academic treatments on the subject and informal, popular discussions.

As an example of the latter, one Baptist leader is fond of saying, "Mama taught me that this is what Baptists have always believed." The premise behind such an approach is that if "mama taught" this or that about Baptists, then it must be true. With all due respect to this person's mother, "mama" may not be right. What is often cited as Baptist precedent is usually tainted by a personal agenda, an ignorance of Baptist history and theology, or some mixture of both. These appeals are based more on emotion than an accurate understanding of the issues. The end result is more confusion or less clarity on the nature of the distinctive identity of Baptists.

Despite the complexity and confusion surrounding the issue of Baptist distinctives, the matter is still one of great importance. These doctrines play a major role in shaping church life and ministry for Baptists. For example, in my own denominational context, considerable debate surrounds the issue of women serving as senior pastor of a church. A Texas Baptist church, associated at that time with the SBC, called a woman to serve as senior pastor. As one might imagine, the actions taken by this church sparked major controversy among Southern Baptists. Interestingly, the issue of Baptist distinctives found its way into the debate.

For example, is a woman serving as pastor of a church faithful to the biblical witness? Is "woman-as-pastor" an issue of biblical authority or biblical interpretation? Is it "baptistic" for a church to call a woman to serve as pastor? Do Southern Baptist churches that have women pastors embody the essence of Baptist life and thought? Does the Baptist distinctive of Christian experience permit a Southern Baptist church to call a woman as pastor? These are only some of the questions often asked whenever this topic is discussed. To summarize the arguments as they relate to the present study, are Southern Baptist churches that call women to serve as pastors true to historical Baptist distinctives?

One strand of Baptist distinctives uses a certain interpretation of Baptist distinctives to answer these questions. They point to doctrines like local church autonomy, soul competency, and individual freedom as the Baptist distinctives that theologically justify a woman serving as senior pastor. After all, God calls and gifts many people for various forms of Christian service, one of which is pastoral ministry. God's calling is sovereign and indiscriminate—that is, he may call whomever he chooses to serve as pastor regardless of gender. God may choose to call and gift either a woman or a man to be a pastor of a Baptist church. If such a person testifies that he or she has experienced such a call, who are we to judge whether this call is valid or invalid? If that person claims to have "experienced" God's call for pastoral ministry, then we must accept that call as true to God's character and word. For some, this line of reasoning fits within the parameters of the previously cited distinctives.

Another group of Baptists adopt a different interpretation of Baptist distinctives to address this issue. These Baptists say that biblical authority and biblical teaching are the absolute and normative standard for interpreting ministry "callings." The Bible specifically stipulates that only men should serve as senior pastor. In addition, the Bible prohibits a woman from serving in such a ministry. Therefore, a woman's "call" to ministry (that is, her experience and interpretation of God's calling) must be interpreted and subordinated to the teachings of the Scriptures. In other words, these Baptists believe that biblical authority is the primary Baptist distinctive, and they use this theological tenet to define who is and who is not qualified to serve in a local church in the office of pastor.

Admittedly, the issue of women serving as pastor is much more complex than this. Historical, theological, and interpretative considerations must have their voices heard in this discussion. Yet, for present purposes, the above account illustrates how closely connected are Baptist perspectives of church and ministry and Baptist distinctives. Baptists use their distinctive identity to shape their ministry within and without local Baptist churches.

Not only do they guide Baptists in their understanding of the nature of the church, but these distinctives also direct ministry relationships with non-Baptist Christian denominations. For example, should Baptist churches unite with non-Baptist Christians for evangelistic and benevolent ministries? If so, which non-Baptist Christian groups are appropriate for such associations and which are not? What would guide Baptists in their search? Can Baptists associate with non-Baptist Christians who have differing views on women's ordination, the mode of baptism, the authority of the Bible, and the qualifications for church membership?

The struggle of various Baptist churches and denominations on many of these issues was evident in the mid-twentieth century as Baptists struggled with whether they should affiliate with the National and World Councils of Churches. Some Baptists joined because they did not believe that the union would compromise their understanding of Baptist distinctives. Other Baptists refused to associate with these organizations because they believed this alliance would undermine or destroy their unique theological identity.

Recent renewed interest further underscores the importance of Baptist distinctives. For example, an unpublished manuscript by Curtis Freeman and others entitled "Re-Envisioning Baptist Identity: A Manifesto for Baptist Communities in North America" argues for a complete re-examination of what should and what should not be regarded as Baptist distinctives. The document critiques past interpretations of Baptist distinctives and proposes a new theological identity and method for Baptists. This treatise is a call to redefine completely the entire theological identity of Baptists.

Also, the Baptist General Convention of Texas organized a commission for the study and development of Baptist distinctives in order to assist Texas Baptists in their understanding of their unique theological identity. The result was a publication by E. Eugene Greer Jr., ed., *Baptists: History, Distinctives, and Relationships* (Dallas: Baptist General Convention of Texas, 1996). The goal of the project was to provide a tool to help Texas SBC churches understand their distinctive theological heritage in order to shape present and future ministry directions. In addition, the entity known as the Cooperative Baptist Fellowship posts on their Internet Web page their interpretation of Baptist distinctives. These and other activities illustrate the continued interest and importance this issue has with Baptists.

The renewed interest in Baptist distinctives in recent days is a welcome development. The past few decades of the twentieth century heard a deafening silence on this issue. One major reason for this may have been the rapid changes that have seized our society. Technological, educational, medical, and other aspects of human life have witnessed incredible transitions occurring at alarming rates. Religious and denominational

changes were no exception. Baptists found themselves address-
ing the implications of all these changes for their own ministries. The rapid sociological changes also brought many
Baptists into new relationships with many non-Baptist
Christians.

Within my own denomination, Southern Baptists have
joined with many non-Baptist evangelicals in new ministry ventures. A new "evangelical ecumenism" has swept over the
Southern Baptist Convention. Areas of commonality and agreement have been identified with many of these and other believers. In pursuing many of these new ventures, however, we have
tended to neglect the traits that have forged our unique theological identity and shaped our mission and passion.

I would suggest that we continue to relate to like-minded
Christians for any and all opportunities to extend the kingdom
of God. As we do this, we should also, as one Baptist of the
past has said so well, "Propagate our Baptist distinctives." This
endeavor is not to proselytize non-Baptists to become Baptists.
Baptists should, however, clearly and unswervingly articulate
their distinctive theological identity. Should these other
Christians become convinced of the "Baptist position," they
would be readily welcomed into the fold.

For the present, the primary emphasis should focus on
preaching, writing, and teaching Baptist distinctives to the
Baptist people. Baptists have always contended that God led
them to discover and develop their theological distinctives.
Baptists have always believed that their distinctives are true to
God's character and accurately reflect what the Bible teaches. If
these are the guiding convictions undergirding Baptist distinctives, then to neglect them is to dishonor God.

THE TASK AT HAND

In light of these considerations, I offer this work on Baptist distinctives. Most treatments of Baptist distinctives, whether writings or sermons, are prescriptive in nature. That is, they offer what the presenter believes to be Baptist distinctives. Little if any attention is given in these examinations to what others may have said on the subject, or if the offered perspective has any connection to other formulations of Baptist distinctives. A few works on Baptist distinctives are thoughtfully constructive and carefully researched. Unfortunately, these are the exception rather than the rule. Most treatments are nothing more than personal opinion that lack critical reflection, theological precision, and historical continuity.

The approach adopted for this study is different from those previously done. I want to do more than develop a brief monograph on my opinion of Baptist distinctives. I want to provide an overview—a survey—of the literature that exists on the subject. What have other Baptists said on this subject? How does a particular writing on Baptist distinctives compare with another? Do similarities exist among the presentations? Are there differences? If so, what are they?

An abundance of materials has been produced over the years giving various options for Baptist distinctives. As far as I know, however, no other work on Baptist distinctives has been developed like this one. This labor began as a dissertation for the requirements of a doctor of philosophy degree. In the process of research, I was amazed to discover that no serious scholarship has ever investigated this subject in this way. No research that I know of has critically analyzed, categorized, and interpreted writings on Baptist distinctives in the following manner.

I hope the following examination infuses an element of objectivity into the discussion on Baptist distinctives. This study could serve as a reference point for defining Baptist distinctives and setting parameters for the subject. We need to separate what are thoughtful discussions on this issue and what are emotional reactions. The following examination hopefully will provide structure and clarification for the debate.

I recognize that Baptist distinctives are developed and shaped by various factors. These influences include historical, geographical, ecumenical, and organizational contexts. For example, a purely historical study could examine how nineteenth-century Baptists developed Baptist distinctives differently from twentieth-century Baptists. Or, another approach could investigate how geographical differences influence the development of Baptist distinctives (i.e., British Baptists versus American Baptists, or Northern Baptists versus Southern Baptists). Further, a study could address how various denominations' entities, such as conventions, unions, conferences, associations, etc., contribute to the formulation of Baptist distinctives.

I am aware of such distinctions and will strive to reflect these differences when they are relevant. These influences, however, are too numerous to be examined in detail in this present undertaking. This omission is not to downplay the importance of these factors. The method of analysis chosen, however, relegates these items beyond the scope of the current investigation. I hope this project serves as a catalyst for future investigation into these important issues. Their impact upon the development of writings on Baptist distinctives merits further inquiry.

The following study examines writings on Baptist distinctives from a literary, historical, and theological analysis. The approach is literary in that it attempts to examine Baptist distinctives as a collective body of literature. Do certain elements define this literature, and, if so, what are they? This study is historical in that the development of certain ideas is traced throughout the continuum of Baptist thought. Particular doctrines are traced through the history of Baptist distinctives to discover major or minor shifts of emphasis. The theological inquiry examines the actual doctrinal content of these works. Comparisons and contrasts of specific doctrines identify areas of theological agreement and disagreement within Baptist thought. The first two chapters of this study are analytical. I look at the materials as a collective whole and seek to interpret the significance of this theological literature in its entirety. The remaining chapters are descriptive. The writings themselves will reveal their unique teachings and emphases.

I have no pretensions that this is the authoritative and final word on the subject. I rather hope that this is the beginning of a broader discussion. Up to this point, the more Baptists discuss their distinctives with others and with themselves, the less uniformity exists. Although somewhat of an exaggeration, Baptists have almost reached the point of no longer having "Baptist distinctives." Instead, each Baptist claims to have his or her own "Baptist distinctives." I do not think that this is an accurate reflection of what it means to be a Baptist, and I certainly do not believe that this growing sentiment accurately reflects our rich tradition as Baptists. Hopefully, what follows in this book will redirect Baptists to reclaim and embrace their collective and unique theological heritage.

The selected bibliography at the end of this book is rather unique. As far as I know, it is the most comprehensive collection of sources on the subject of Baptist distinctives. Most of the formal treatises claiming in some fashion to be a full treatment on the subject are listed. Although limited in number, I have also included secondary sources that in some measure supplement or enhance the discussion. Other works that have in some way supported or shaped the research for this project are also mentioned. If this project offers nothing else of value, the bibliography is a useful contribution to Baptist distinctives.

CHAPTER ONE

Defining Baptist Distinctive Genre

Baptists believe and affirm many doctrines. Some of these are specifically "baptistic" and some are not. We must recognize that part of Baptist beliefs are those doctrines that are shared with all orthodox Christians. These convictions include concepts such as God as Trinity and the person and work of Jesus Christ. On these and other issues, there is not a distinctively Baptist position.

Within the broad spectrum of Baptist life there are convictions that are unique only to Baptists. These tenets will be the focus of our attention. Most agree that Baptists have a distinctive theological identity. Few agree, however, on the nature of this identity. The problem is compounded when seeking to find this identity. Where exactly should one look to discover the distinctive beliefs of Baptists?

Baptists express their theological identity in numerous ways. They produce works that examine single issues, such as the doctrines of salvation or creation. Baptists develop systematic theologies that examine the major doctrines of the Christian faith in a coherent, thematic fashion. Baptists are also a people of social conscience, and they often express that conscience in writings that address ethical issues, such as gambling, world hunger, substance abuse, genetic engineering, etc. These and other types of writings, when produced by Baptists, may or may not have a Baptist slant to their perspective. While useful in understanding Baptists, these kinds of writings cannot be considered works on Baptist distinctives. They do not communicate intentionally the unique beliefs of Baptists.

In the following discussion, I will tackle two major problems identified in the study of Baptist distinctives. First, I will address the subject of definition. What are the raw materials, the elements that constitute Baptist distinctives? Are there identifiable theological ideas that define Baptist distinctives and other ideas that do not? If so, what are these beliefs? Defining the nature of Baptist distinctives will hopefully address these and similar questions. The second issue I will examine is function. What do writings on Baptist distinctives attempt to accomplish? What purpose do Baptist distinctives serve? Determining the function of Baptist distinctives will enhance our understanding of their purpose.

The approach I have adopted for the following examination is to treat writings on Baptist distinctives as a unique form of literature, a theological genre. The word *genre* means that, within theological studies, there exists a distinct class of writings that collectively form a body of literature called Baptist distinctives. I will use the term *genre* to describe this collection of theological literature.

DEFINING BAPTIST DISTINCTIVES

In my analysis of writings on Baptist distinctives, I have discovered four broad theological components. These elements are present in all writings on Baptist distinctives and are definitive for this genre; that is, they define what is and what is not a writing on Baptist distinctives. After critically examining hundreds of documents, I conclude all writings that qualify as Baptist distinctive genre contain the following theological traits. These components are: the epistemological, the polemical, the ecclesiological, and the volitional.

EPISTEMOLOGICAL COMPONENT

The first element in Baptist distinctive writings is the epistemological component. Epistemology is the inquiry into how knowledge is gained. It is a concern for the basis of religious knowledge—in this particular case, the basis for the theological claims of Baptist distinctives. These writings are careful to establish the authoritative foundation for the distinctive theology of Baptists. The credibility of the theology of Baptist distinctives is intricately tied to the trustworthiness of the foundation for those theological claims. All writings that qualify as Baptist distinctives demonstrate this vital concern for a solid epistemology.

This concept has two different expressions: biblical authority and Christian experience. Biblical authority is the notion that the Bible in some way serves as the authoritative basis for the theology of Baptist distinctives. Christian experience is the idea that an individual religious experience of God is the foundation for the unique doctrines of Baptists. I will examine the authority of the distinctive theology of Baptists under these two categories.

Biblical Authority. The most prominent basis for religious authority within Baptist distinctives is the Bible. Along with other Christian denominations, Baptists appeal to the Bible as their ultimate, or sole, source for theology. Baptists distance themselves from others, however, by claiming a complete dependence upon Scripture as the principal foundation for belief and practice. Whereas other Christian groups incorporate sources for religious authority such as tradition and experience, Baptists in their distinctive writings contend that they alone consistently regard the Bible as their religious authority. Baptists aim to restore the order of the primitive churches. They make no appeal to tradition, the Fathers, or expediency. They simply ask, "What do the Scriptures teach?" They follow the New Testament model of a church and invite all to test them by it. It is not strange, therefore, that they confidently appeal to God's Word for proof of the correctness of all they do. They take it all from the Bible, and therefore they know it can all be found there. Take any Scripture account of the course pursued by the apostles, or of the practice of gospel churches, and you will find the counterpart in a Baptist church.[1]

While some within this group argue for the entire Bible, another segment limits the religious authority of Baptist distinctives to the New Testament.

It is this emphasis on the supremacy of the New Testament in all matters of the Church's faith and practice that constitutes the basis of the Baptist position. It is to the New Testament we must go for direction, and it is by the standards of the New Testament that we must seek to regulate our convictions and conduct.[2]

Those Baptists who cling to this idea argue that this strict adherence to the New Testament is distinctive only of Baptists. "When Baptists say that the New Testament is the only law for Christian institutions they part company, if not theoretically at least practically, with most of the Protestant world, as well as from the Greeks and Romanists."[3] Some Baptists teach that doctrines should not be considered "baptistic" if they are neither found in nor supported by the New Testament.[4]

One evidence of the important role the Bible has in the distinctive genre is revealed in the way in which doctrines are developed. Considerable effort is often given to careful interpretation of certain Scriptures in order to develop or substantiate a particular theological point.

Biblical authority is of paramount importance for the development of doctrine in distinctive writings. Baptists resolutely oppose any authoritative imposition between God and man. Such intrusions interfere with the faith relationship between the Creator and his creation. Because of this aversion, Baptists oppose certain uses of creedal statements. *Creeds* are summaries of the beliefs of a particular Christian denomination. Instead of appealing to creeds as the authoritative basis for theological development, Baptists claim the Scriptures as their rule for all matters of conviction and conduct.

Baptists have historically rejected particular uses of creeds. For example, they have rejected any creedalism where the government attempts to regulate or coerce religion or faith. Baptists also have repudiated any creedalism that elevates manmade interpretations equal to or above biblical authority. They interpret these kinds of creedalism as attempts to replace God's authority with human authority.

Opposition to these sorts of creedalism, however, is not the same as a "voluntary, conscientious adherence to explicit doctrinal statements."[5] Baptists have supported the usage of certain statements to express their doctrinal identity and have even used the term *creed* to describe the practice. This use of creedalism does not undermine the superlative position the Bible enjoys in Baptist life. In fact, this expression of creedalism is found in some Baptist distinctive writings.

Christian Experience. A second basis for religious authority is Christian experience. While the majority of distinctive writings argue for biblical authority, a smaller group contends that Christian experience should serve as the basis for the distinctive theology of Baptists. The argument is that a Christian cannot have a valid understanding of the Bible and conversion without first having experienced God. E. Y. Mullins is a prominent Baptist who represents this line of thought.[6]

The point I want to make here is that one of these two expressions of the epistemological component exists in these writings. I will address the specific content of these items later. For the moment, I am simply stipulating that all writings on Baptist distinctives are concerned about the foundation for theological claims.

POLEMICAL COMPONENT

The second major component found in these writings is polemical intention. Polemical intention is the notion that an author is deliberately developing the theological traits that he believes distinguishes Baptists from other Christians. The polemic is the purposeful critique of other denominations in light of their differences with Baptists. This concept is essential for writings on Baptist distinctives because it is a major element that sets these writings apart from other types of Baptist theological works.

Polemical intention is theologically concerned and directed toward various issues. The polemic typically criticizes the authoritative basis of the doctrines of non-Baptist Christians.

The differences of these other groups are often judged deficient in light of the Baptist position on the issue. The goal of this effort is to highlight the supremacy and uniqueness of the distinctives of Baptists.

The polemic takes various shapes in Baptist distinctives. Particular doctrines such as the practice of infant baptism, state-established churches, grace conveyed through religious rituals by specially ordained priests, religious traditions, and noncongregational church government have felt the brunt of the Baptist polemic. Baptists have criticized specific denominations such as Roman Catholics, Episcopalians, Congregationalists, Methodists, Presbyterians, Lutherans, and Campbellites. Certain religious movements have also been castigated, including the National and World Council of Churches. Baptists have on occasion reproved themselves.[7]

ECCLESIOLOGICAL COMPONENT

The third item that defines distinctive writings is the ecclesiological component. Ecclesiology is the study and practice of the doctrine of the church. Baptist distinctive writings always reflect great concern for the church. Whenever an author is developing Baptist distinctives, the doctrine of the church is always present. In fact, one could argue that Baptists best express their theology within the nature and ministries of a Baptist church. In a sense, Baptist distinctive theology "lives" in the Baptist church. The Baptist church is, therefore, the most visible expression of those elements that distinguish Baptists from other Christian denominations.

One evidence of this attribute is the doctrine of baptism. With regard to the mode, Baptists maintain that the proper expression of baptism found in the New Testament is immersion. Baptists consistently affirm the importance of the meaning contained in immersion. Some distinctive writings so emphasize the importance of baptism by immersion that the Lord's Supper is denied to those who have not been baptized in this way.[8] Not only is the mode of baptism discussed, but so also is the meaning. Believer's baptism is the baptism of conscious believers capable of exercising their will. Baptists contend that this meaning of baptism is what distinguishes Baptists from other Christians, specifically those who practice infant baptism. While insisting that baptism is unnecessary for salvation, Baptists maintain that it is important and necessary for church membership.[9]

The doctrine of a regenerate church is another indicator of this concept. Baptists state that a visible, local church should only have as members those persons who have experienced God's grace through faith, have been baptized, and voluntarily associate and participate with the local church. This idea is different from the doctrine of a state church. In this paradigm, all who live within a certain geographical area are members of the church. Conversion is not essential for church membership in the state church model. For Baptists, this perspective undermines the very heart of the gospel. They argue that only born-again, baptized believers should be members of a church.[10]

Congregational church government is another expression of the ecclesiological component. Baptists readily admit that congregational polity is not their sole theological property. They do claim, however, to make a novel contribution to the doctrine by joining believer's baptism together with soul competency to form a distinctive church government. This arrangement of doctrines permits Baptists to claim that their view of church government is unique to them.[11]

VOLITIONAL COMPONENT

The fourth trait common in all writings on Baptist distinctives is the volitional component. This element is expressed in two concepts that are similar yet distinct: religious liberty and soul competency.

The designation of religious liberty and soul competency under the notion "volition" follows that established by E. Y. Mullins in *The Axioms of Religion: A New Interpretation of the Baptist Identity.* Although Mullins does give two separate discussions of the topics, the ideas have some overlap of meaning in writings on Baptist distinctives. Mullins joins the concepts of freedom and responsibility together. For him, every individual is made in the image of God and is therefore competent, responsible, and accountable to deal personally with God. Individual, or "soul," competency further implies an unhindered access to receive or to reject a personal, individual relationship with God. Each person is obligated to address his or her spiritual standing before God.

Further, society is obligated to provide an unhindered or unobtrusive environment to allow persons the freedom to deal with God in this way. This rationale is why Mullins includes both soul competency and religious freedom together in his discussion. Because Mullins gave these two ideas an overlapping treatment within the general confines of his discussion, I am including the concepts under one major heading.[12]

One expression of the volitional component is religious liberty. Baptists lived as a disadvantaged and persecuted sect for hundreds of years in England and in colonial America. Due to these circumstances, Baptists constantly cried out for the freedom to follow their religious convictions and beliefs without external interference.

Religious liberty was a revolutionary idea during the first centuries of Baptist life. Not only did Baptists include their sentiments on this subject in separate treatises and confessions of faith, but they also treated it extensively in their distinctive writings. The reason for their insistence on religious freedom is attributed to their understanding of the gospel as requiring a voluntary, intentional response without external coercion. As a distinctive expression of their unique theological identity, Baptists assert that the essence of their tradition is that faith must be a free and voluntary response to God.[13]

Another expression of the volitional component is soul competency. Because of the inherent connection between the two ideas, when Baptists contend for religious freedom, they normally discuss soul competency. Baptists adamantly hold to the notion that an individual has the ability and responsibility to approach God directly without any human intermediary. In American Baptist life, soul competency has penetrated deeply into the distinctive theological identity of Baptists.[14]

THE FUNCTION OF BAPTIST DISTINCTIVES

The next phase in our examination of the genre of Baptist distinctives identifies their function. The method I have adopted for doing this is to place this body of writings within already established categories of theology. The possible options for this are: biblical, systematic, philosophical, and historical theologies. Determining which of these options best describes writings on Baptist distinctives will help decide the purpose of these writings.

There are several definitions for biblical theology. The one most relevant for our discussion is that biblical theology is a theology based on the Bible.[15] This perspective is different from those theologies that include philosophical conceptions or religious traditions. As already demonstrated, Baptist distinctive writings are quite concerned to be biblical in their theology. Numerous works on Baptist distinctives expend great effort to establish the biblical foundation for some particular doctrine.

Some distinctive works even argue for certain kinds of biblical interpretative methods. Many of the elements within Baptist distinctives are based on the Bible and are biblical in their orientation. The theological components, however, are too diverse in their scope to fit exclusively within the parameters of biblical theology.

Systematic theology is the orderly presentation of the doctrines of the Christian faith. This discipline primarily uses the Bible for theological construction. Other sources, such as church history and philosophy, are also used in subordination to the Bible when appropriate to do so. Systematic theology is concerned with integrating all Christian doctrine in a coherent manner for a contemporary expression of the Christian faith.[16] As I will demonstrate later, Baptist distinctives are quite concerned with presenting their theology coherently. They are systematic in the formulation and integration of their doctrines. As a category, however, systematic theology is too encompassing to describe accurately the distinctive theology of Baptists.

Philosophical theology is a discipline that examines the ideas, truth claims, and methods utilized in a theological discipline. Philosophical theology can defend and scrutinize theological claims. Some even use philosophy inappropriately to supply content for theology.[17] It is naïve to think that Baptist distinctives were formulated in a philosophical vacuum, void of any influences from the prevailing thought structures of the day. Further, the polemical component functions philosophically as it scrutinizes and defends theology. Philosophical theology, however, cannot account for all the doctrinal components contained in writings on Baptist distinctives. This category is therefore inadequate to describe the function of Baptist distinctives.

A final possibility for our categorization of Baptist distinctives is historical theology. Several understandings for this field of study exist. The definition that I have adopted for this investigation is the treatment of doctrinal developments according to major confessional traditions. These traditions include Eastern Orthodox, Roman Catholic, and Protestant. The approach examines theological movements, key thinkers, major church councils, and creeds for each of the confessional traditions. Theological implications are often developed for contemporary belief and practice.[18]

I contend that the unique theological literature known as Baptist distinctives should be categorized under this latter branch of theological studies. As such, I am going to treat writings on Baptist distinctives as a form of confessional theology within the broader stream of historical theology.

Before specifically examining Baptist distinctives as confessional theology, we need to clarify a few terms. The first of these is the word *confessionalism*. Confessionalism has several nuanced understandings. I believe it is helpful to see these slight distinctions because, in a sense, all these feed into the definition I will use.

One form of confessionalism is simply the production of confessions of faith. Confessions of faith are theological documents that provide doctrinal identity and promote denominational unity.[19] In one sense, Baptist distinctives serve this purpose. Confessions of faith differ from Baptist distinctives, however, in that the former also identifies common areas of belief that Baptists share with other Christian denominations. As already demonstrated, Baptist distinctives are not overly concerned to show areas of agreement with other Christians. Instead, distinctive writings develop the theological features that distinguish Baptists from others. So this form of confessionalism, while similar, is also different.

Another understanding of confessionalism is the formal presentation of beliefs produced by Protestants. These presentations provide interpretive guides to Scripture, usually expounding the recognized creed of faith of a particular denomination. Confessionalism in this sense produces formal theological treatises that are classified as "confessional theologies." These confessional theologies normally profess a Protestant understanding of the Reformed faith, usually in opposition to Roman Catholicism.[20]

Again, there is a sense in which this perspective feeds into the approach I have chosen. Baptist distinctives do provide limited guidance for Baptist understandings on certain doctrinal issues. And they typically do profess a certain perspective that is usually distinct from other Christian traditions, including other Protestant groups and Roman Catholicism. Baptist distinctives do not, however, profess only an exclusive Reformed theology. Further, they only develop the distinctive theology of Baptists. They do not describe exhaustively all the doctrines of Baptists. Since Baptists do not possess formally adopted creeds of faith as do some other Protestant denominations, these distinctive writings are not interpretative guides to such documents.

The two previous understandings of confessionalism converge into a position proposed by Martin Cook. I have adopted Cook's approach as a means for understanding Baptist distinctives as confessional theology. Cook suggests that a confessional theology should derive its core insights and its theological "starting point" from the unique perspective of one Christian denomination. This theological development may or may not interpret the formal creedal statements of a particular denomination.[21] In the case of Baptists, there is no formal creed to interpret. Cook's perspective, however, does permit production of confessional theologies, even without creeds of faith.

Cook's understanding provides the best categorization and explanation of the function of Baptist distinctives. Adopting his general framework, I have identified three major criteria that permit Baptist distinctives to be classified as a form of confessional theology. The first of the criteria is a "cognizant awareness" in which a particular doctrinal position is constructed. A confessional theology has an inherent intention to formulate theological claims within one specific denomination.

A second consideration is the "analytical endeavor." Confessional theologies define the doctrinal foundation for the unique perspective of the specific denomination. It also identifies the doctrinal bases of other denominations. The analytical endeavor answers questions such as: What is the basis of our theology? What is the basis of the theology of other denominations? How do we do our theology? How do other denominations construct their theology? Confessional theologies grapple with the inner workings of the theological development of its own heritage as well as those of other Christian communities.

A final point of a confessional theology is "dialectic interaction." Dialectic interaction is the comparison of one's own unique theological identity with another Christian community of faith. The results of this process are varied. Sometimes the comparison is simply a description without any critical judgments on the merits of the positions. Sometimes the comparison will advocate the superiority of one theological position over another denomination's perspective, or the analysis may attempt a synthesis of the positions examined.

CONCLUSION

Based upon the previous criteria, I contend that writings on Baptist distinctives should be classified as confessional theology under the broader discipline of historical theology. These writings reflect a cognizant awareness of the Baptist community in which they are developed. The unique theological identity of Baptists is formulated within the Baptist community. Writings on Baptist distinctives attempt to preserve and foster the distinctive theological identity of Baptists. Distinctive writings incorporate the first element of confessional theology.

Baptist distinctives also conform to the analytical endeavor. Distinctive writings attempt to establish a credible basis on which to construct their distinctive theology. This foundation is either biblical authority or Christian experience, depending upon which particular Baptist distinctive writing a person is reading. As previously mentioned, these documents compare and contrast the basis for the theological claims of Baptist with other Christian denominations. Baptist distinctive writings therefore conform to the second element of confessional theology.

The trait of dialectic interaction is also present in the literature. The distinctive genre typically compares the content and method of the unique theology of Baptists with other Christian communities of faith. The Baptist comparison is more than mere description. The comparison never seeks a synthesis of the positions examined. The dialectic interaction typically advocates the superiority of the Baptist position over other denominations. Writings on Baptist distinctives therefore adhere to the third aspect of confessional theology.

This understanding of confessional theology provides a category that best describes the function of this body of theological literature. The purpose of Baptist distinctives is to articulate and preserve the unique theological identity of Baptists. Distinctive writings identify and define the peculiar doctrines of Baptists. They do so with the distinct awareness of the Baptist heritage. They interact critically with other Christian traditions, affirming the superiority of the unique theological identity of Baptists over other Christian denominations.

I conclude from the previous discussion that Baptists have a definitive, confessional theological tradition. This tradition is a clearly identifiable body of literature, a genre, and is comprised of certain theological components that must be present in order to be classified as a distinctive writing. The components share doctrinal emphases that are present to some degree in all writings on Baptist distinctives. The expressions "Baptist confessional theology" or "Baptist confessional tradition" are accurate and appropriate phrases to refer to this category of theology.

Since Baptists do possess a confessional theological tradition, I want to make several observations regarding its doctrinal significance for Baptists.

First, this distinctive tradition may be used to identify and define the theological essence of Baptists. Being "Baptist" is more than just a name. Baptists have been and should be known by clearly defined and historically established theological components. Baptists are more than just defenders of religious freedom, advocates of baptism via immersion, or practitioners of congregational polity. Baptists are those individuals and churches that embrace to some degree all the core theological components that have been identified as common in writings on Baptist distinctives. For a person or church simply to advocate one or two of the theological components does not designate that person or church as "Baptist." Whenever an individual or church deviates from one or more of these theological components, they deviate from the historically established boundaries that define Baptists.

Another observation is that Baptists have a continuous theological identity. Baptist distinctives reflect diversity of emphasis in their doctrinal expressions. These differences may be shaped by a variety of historical, contextual, and theological influences. The differences are surpassed, however, by greater theological concerns. Baptist distinctives share common theological conceptions that are present in all distinctive writings.

In other words, contemporary Baptists support certain doctrinal convictions that were espoused by Baptists in previous centuries. When viewed from this perspective, Baptists have a common theological tradition that ties them together around a core theological identity. Some may change nuances of meaning or arrangement of the components, but they cannot change the presence or the essential nature of the distinctives and still remain within the confessional tradition of Baptists. The fact that Baptists adhere to certain distinctive doctrinal traits is an affirmation of the theological adequacy of these traits. These convictions transcend cultural and historical differences and bind Baptists to established theological components.

A third observation is that the theological commonality shared among Baptists in no way diminishes the theological diversity found in Baptist theology. This continuous theological tradition strengthens the notion that Baptist distinctives furnish a shared theological identity while simultaneously providing a basis from which to address the contextual, historical, and theological concerns that confront differing Baptists in differing times and contexts. In other words, a Baptist confessional tradition supplies doctrinal continuity so that Baptists can formulate their doctrinal conceptions within the well-established parameters of the Baptist confessional tradition. The confessional tradition likewise provides enormous flexibility, allowing Baptists to address specific cultural concerns and contemporary issues theologically while permitting the formulators to remain within the Baptist confessional tradition.

CHAPTER TWO

Formation of Doctrine

The next item of examination in our analysis of Baptist distinctives is the development of doctrine. I want to investigate the manner in which Baptist distinctives construct their theology. Each writing on Baptist distinctives develops a defining, core distinctive. This core distinctive serves as an interpretative guide that influences and shapes the other distinctives. I recognize that Baptists and their distinctive theology are far too diverse to be reduced to a single theological trait. In fact, some scholars claim that writings on Baptist distinctives do not have an organizing principle.[1] The evidence, however, persuades me otherwise. One of the strongest arguments in favor of using a core distinctive to develop the other components is that many authors of Baptist distinctives admit that this is what they are doing.

As I mentioned in the last chapter, the epistemological component has two different expressions in Baptist distinctive genre: biblical authority and Christian experience. Writings on Baptist distinctives use one of these two elements as the interpretative distinctive to formulate the other distinctives. I will follow this twofold designation as we explore the manner in which these theological treatises construct their theology.

BIBLICAL AUTHORITY

The first category uses biblical authority as its defining distinctive. Biblical authority is found in three different guises in the distinctive genre. These are: the authority of the Bible, a regenerate church membership, and baptism by immersion.[2]

THE AUTHORITY OF THE BIBLE

This first group argues that the interpretative distinctive for Baptists is the authority of the Bible as the foundation for Christian belief. This category insists that other Christian denominations, though formally asserting this principle, either intentionally or unintentionally elevate other sources of authority to equal status as the Bible. These writings argue that Baptists are the most consistent and committed to the notion that the Bible is the final standard for religious authority.

The authority of the Bible has multiple expressions. Some distinctive writings advocate the "sole" authority of the Bible, while another group supports the "supreme" authority of the Scriptures. The Bible as the sole authority suggests that the Scriptures are the exclusive authority for matters of faith and practice. Supreme authority means that the Bible is the highest level of authority and ranks above the church, religious tradition, or any other source that might have some measure of religious authority.

These two groups reflect some measure of difference in their understanding of the Bible's authority. The similarities of theological expression, however, far outweigh any differences and allow for the inclusion of the two together. Both groups have biblical authority as the interpretative component. Further, both groups state that Baptists are the most consistent in relegating the Bible to this authoritative role. Finally, both sole and supreme authority advocates argue that this unwavering fidelity to the Bible for faith and practice is unique to Baptists.

This category of Baptist distinctives maintains that the authoritative role of the Bible best accounts for the distinctive theological characteristics of Baptists. Writings on Baptist distinctives propose one of two possibilities for the interpretative component. The authority of the Bible is the most prevalent and dominant core component among all writings on Baptist distinctives.

REGENERATE CHURCH MEMBERSHIP

The doctrine of a regenerate church membership is another evidence of the core component of biblical authority. A regenerate church membership stipulates that a person must be born again before he or she can rightfully be considered a member of a local church. This perspective begins with the notion that the Holy Spirit has created a new, spiritual life in a sinner. This regenerating work of God qualifies that person for membership in a local church.

Baptist distinctive writings in this category assert that local congregations should be composed only of those persons who are converted, have received baptism by immersion, and agree freely to participate in the life of a local church. These assertions stand in contrast to all-inclusive state churches. Baptists, maybe more than any other Christian denomination, deplore the spiritual state of inclusive state churches. A regenerate church membership doctrine is one attempt by Baptists to ensure a pure church.

One could argue that the distinctive component of a regenerate church membership should be classified under Christian experience rather than biblical authority. Concepts such as conversion, baptism, and participation in church life all assume the doctrine of a regenerate church membership. Further, these items are somewhat experiential in nature and expression.

Within this category, however, writers on Baptist distinctives formulate their understandings of a church membership not in terms of experience, but rather in terms of biblical authority. Two examples demonstrate this affinity. T. T. Eaton begins his discussion of Baptist distinctives by acknowledging that all Baptist doctrines are "corollaries" of the Baptist view of "absolute submission to Scripture teaching."[3] Eaton then proposes three prominent points "on which Baptists differ from other denominations." These are ideas that he develops from the prior notion of biblical authority.

The first of these points, and the one most relevant for our current discussion, is the idea of a regenerate church membership. Eaton argues that a regenerate church membership is a primary trait of the Baptist distinctive genre. What Eaton has done is to argue a particular doctrine (regenerate church membership) from a prior assumption of authority (biblical authority). I conclude that, for Eaton, the doctrine of a regenerate church membership is a tangible expression of the prior assumption of biblical authority.

Norman Maring and Winthrop S. Hudson also exemplify this practice. These authors propose that the doctrine of a regenerate church membership is the most distinctive trait of Baptist theology.[4] Their rationale for this assertion, however, is derived from "the Scriptures which testify to God's intention in Christ." Their understanding of a regenerate church membership is therefore derived from their prior assumption of biblical authority. This is further evidenced in their theological exposition of select biblical passages that support their perspective. Again, this doctrine is based upon the notion that the Bible is the authority for theological construction. I contend that this demonstrates that the doctrine of a regenerate church membership is a subtle expression of biblical authority.

BAPTISM BY IMMERSION

Another evidence of the core component of biblical authority is baptism by immersion. This particular doctrinal expression, as a core component within the distinctive genre, is almost nonexistent in contemporary Baptist life. It is more commonly found in Baptist distinctive writings developed in the nineteenth century, most notably among Landmark Baptists. Because this particular doctrinal expression is present within this genre, I think its presence merits at least some treatment.

Among its many tenets, Landmark Baptists essentially believed that the only true church in existence was the Baptist church. Baptism by immersion was a visible expression of the authenticity and authority of Baptist churches. For these Baptists, immersion was the essential expression of the nature of conversion and the nature of the church. This doctrine became a defining principle for participation in church life. If an individual was not baptized by immersion in a local Baptist church, that person was not considered a member in a New Testament church. Baptism by immersion was the trait that distinguished a true church from a mere religious organization.[5]

Baptism by immersion as a core component is developed much like the doctrine of a regenerate church membership. J. M. Pendleton, for example, argues that his understanding of

baptism by immersion as the core distinctive has its "foundation in the word of God."[6] Because the Bible forms the authoritative basis for this doctrine, Baptists should adhere to it with
"unswerving fidelity." Immersion thus assumes the prior theological conviction of biblical authority. I conclude that the core
distinctive of baptism by immersion is in essence another
expression of biblical authority.

CHRISTIAN EXPERIENCE

Biblical authority was the first core distinctive for Baptists.
With the dawn of the twentieth century, another organizing principle was developed as the core theological distinctive. E. Y.
Mullins, in his influential work *Axioms of Religion: A New
Interpretation of the Baptist Faith,* argued that Christian experience (i.e., soul competency) should serve as the core component
for developing Baptist distinctives. Mullins's development of
Christian experience birthed a new tradition of Baptist distinctive
writings The result was a new tradition of Baptist distinctives.

Christian experience now stands alongside biblical authority as a defining distinctive. Like the core component of biblical authority, Christian experience is found in several forms.
These are: soul competency, religious freedom, believer's baptism, and the lordship of Christ.

SOUL COMPETENCY

Soul competency is the right and ability of an individual to
approach God directly without any human intermediary.
Further, "the principle of soul competency assumes that man is
made in God's image, and that God is a person able to reveal
himself to man, and God can communicate with man" directly.
This encounter occurs within the context of Christian religious
experience.

Soul competency affirms that all persons have an inalienable right of access to God. This direct access results in either a personal acceptance or rejection of God. In other words, because all persons are created in the image of God, they stand in a unique relationship to their Creator. They are "competent" to deal directly with God. When the heart of an individual is quickened by God's grace, the individual responds experientially to God. Reception of God, through the initiative of grace, allows the person to approach the Creator without a human intermediary. Conversely, individuals are fully competent, or capable, of rejecting God. Soul competency applies equally to all sentient persons. Every individual is responsible to God for his or her relationship to him. This competent accountability occurs within the context of a person's religious experience.

RELIGIOUS FREEDOM

Some Baptists consider religious freedom to be the core distinctive.[7] The reason I include this concept within the broader category of Christian experience is that the distinctive genre typically clusters several experiential concepts together. Discussions of soul competency naturally lead into discussions of religious freedom, and treatments of religious freedom normally include examinations of soul competency.[8]

Religious freedom asserts that the human, temporal realm has no authority to coerce religious commitments. God alone is sovereign over human conscience. Religious freedom guarantees the right of each individual to believe as he or she chooses without fear of penalty. This kind of freedom also ensures that all religious congregations have the opportunity to structure their own faith and practice in accordance with their understanding of divine truth.

This conviction was birthed by Baptists who lived as an oppressed and persecuted group of Christians for centuries, constantly seeking relief from their tormentors. These Baptists fought for religious freedom in order to protect the right of every person to serve or reject God. Religious freedom ensured the opportunity to follow one's conscience regarding religious convictions and practices without fear of external interference. The goal was to promote genuinely pure, regenerate churches and sincerity in the individual's religious experience.

BELIEVER'S BAPTISM

Another example of the core distinctive of Christian experience is believer's baptism. Baptists who believe that this is the organizing principle argue that the voluntary baptism of a sentient person is an indication of a true conversion experience, thereby differentiating Baptists from other Christian groups. This rite marked a person's entrance into the church. Believer's baptism is a "central truth of permanent importance." It means that an individual is professing a voluntary experience of a personal, uncoerced faith in God. It portrays "the right of the soul to an immediate relation to God."[9] This practice is presented as the essence of a true, religious experience. For this reason, few other traits in Baptist life and thought have received as much attention or required as much defense as this doctrine.

H. Wheeler Robinson may offer the best example of believer's baptism as the defining Baptist distinctive. His understanding of believer's baptism is significant because of its strong experiential emphasis. Robinson stipulates that religious experience is a prior principle behind his interpretation of this doctrine. He notes that "the emphasis on experience which characterizes the Baptist faith" finds its expression "in the retention of the baptism of believer's only."[10] For Robinson, believer's baptism finds its spiritual authority in one's conscious acceptance of Christ's authority, a personal submission to that authority, and the individual's commitment to this authority.[11]

Robinson seems to argue that authority is something that occurs within the context of individual experience. He makes no mention of authority existing apart or independent of a person and their religious experience.

This particular understanding illustrates the individual and experiential nature of believer's baptism in Robinson's thought. This contention is further demonstrated in that Robinson connects his understanding of individual autonomy with Mullins's understanding of soul competency and religious experience. Robinson therefore derives his understanding of believer's baptism from his understanding of religious experience. These considerations justify categorizing his work within this section of Christian experience.

THE LORDSHIP OR SOVEREIGNTY OF CHRIST

Baptists do not claim that the lordship of Christ is their exclusive theological property. Select Baptists do, however, argue that this doctrine is the primary distinctive of Baptists. They argue that Baptists have a more "radical dedication to this cardinal truth of Christianity" than other Christian groups.

The exact classification of this particular doctrine was somewhat difficult. I considered designating the lordship of Christ as a third major category. This would have resulted in three major distinctive traditions: biblical authority, Christian experience, and the lordship of Christ. Three reasons, however, led me to include this doctrine within the category of Christian experience.

First, the manner in which this doctrine is constructed led me to include it under the category of Christian experience. The lordship of Christ contains two essential ingredients: an objective element and a subjective element. The objective element is Christ's ruling, or sovereignty, over all things. This rule is absolute. Whether an individual personally experiences Christ's lordship is irrelevant; Jesus Christ is still Lord over all of creation. The subjective element is the personal appropriation of Christ's rule in the hearts and lives of individual believers. This personal appropriation occurs within the context of a person's religious experience with Christ.

Of significance for our discussion is this: Which of these elements, objective or subjective, is commonly found in distinctive genre? Writers of Baptist distinctives who argue for the lordship of Christ as the primary distinctive emphasize the subjective element. This group builds its understanding on the individual's experience of Christ or one's personal encounter with God. This language demonstrates an experiential emphasis. Typically in distinctive genre, when the objective nature of some doctrine is discussed, some kind of biblical exposition occurs, or biblical citations are given. This would be an objective emphasis. Discussions of biblical authority or basing Christ's lordship on biblical treatment are missing in these writings. If the proponents of this position had wanted to emphasize the objective nature of Christ's lordship, it seems to me that they would have based their argument on biblical texts or biblical exposition. These distinctive writings did not use this approach.

A second reason for the classification of Christ's lordship under Christian experience is the time period when this emphasis first appears. No writings on Baptist distinctives seem to argue for this doctrine as the core distinctive prior to the twentieth century. The rise of this tenet seems to have occurred in conjunction with the experiential emphasis developed and established by E. Y. Mullins. I will say more on Mullins and his impact upon Baptist distinctives in a later chapter.

Finally, the manner in which this doctrine is presented led me to include it under Christian experience. Those writings that contend for Christ's lordship as the core distinctive do so in strongly experiential language. For example, John D. Freeman stipulates that the core "Baptist principle" is "an acute and vivid consciousness of the sovereignty of Christ, accompanied by a steadfast determination to secure the complete and consistent recognition of His personal, direct and unrelegated authority" over the soul of the individual. Freeman then states that his understanding of "Christ's sovereignty" is the direct corollary of "religious experience." In doing this, Freeman not only discusses this doctrine using individual, experiential language, but he also seems to limit Christ's lordship to the individual's religious experience.[12]

Another example can be found in James D. Mosteller. He contends that the essence of Christ's lordship is in a personal, experiential union between the believer and the living Christ. Mosteller suggests that Christ's lordship must remain a direct, unmediated relationship between Christ and the believer. Any barriers or impediments that would hinder, jeopardize, or negate the experiential nature of this direct, personal rule must be rejected.[13] As was the case with Freeman, Mosteller uses highly experiential language to discuss Christ's lordship. He also closely connects Christ's lordship to soul competency and religious freedom, both of which I have previously classified under Christian experience. Based on these considerations, it seems logical to me to locate the writings that argue for Christ's lordship as the core distinctive under the category of Christian experience.

This group of distinctive genre argues that Christianity is essentially a personal, experiential religion. The Christian religion is that of a person, namely Christ, and that one embraces the Christian religion in an individual experience of God through Christ. No church or religious institution can mediate in these matters of faith and practice. "No elaborate, impersonal system of rites, ceremonies, and external forms must be permitted to come between the soul and the Savior."[14] The person of

Christ and the authority of his will are realized within the context of the person's individual experience of him. The experience of Christ's authority must remain immediate and undelegated.

TWO DISTINCTIVE TRADITIONS

Writings on Baptist distinctives have different interpretative distinctives that influence their theological emphases. Baptist distinctives writings that affirm biblical authority as the core distinctive begin with some assertion of the importance of the Bible as the foundation for the other distinctives. The tendency to use biblical authority to develop the other Baptist distinctives reflects the Protestant Reformation tradition of asserting the objective authority of the Bible from which other doctrines are developed. In fact, many of the authors of Baptist distinctives state that Baptists and their distinctive theory are the logical outcome of the Reformation Principle of *Sola Scriptura*. *Sola Scriptura* is the idea that the Scriptures, and not human authority or tradition, are alone authoritative for faith and practice. This strand of distinctive writings is called the "Reformation tradition" of Baptist distinctives.

Writings on Baptist distinctives that affirm the primacy of Christian experience embrace assumptions of the philosophical movement known as the Enlightenment. The Enlightenment was a philosophical movement of the eighteenth century. Among its many emphases was the idea of the complete autonomy of each individual. The Enlightenment's philosophical premises, such as autonomous moral agency, strict individualism, and self-evident assertions of human freedom, are embodied in the strand of distinctive writings that use Christian experience as the core distinctive. This tradition of Enlightenment distinctives, which began with Mullins's *The Axioms of Religion,* continues to reflect this theological disposition.

The Reformation tradition begins with biblical authority. From this foundation, these writings formulate a Baptist ecclesiology that is consistent with biblical teaching. The volitional components of soul competency, Christian experience, and religious freedom are necessary corollaries to construct a doctrine of the church that is true to the Scriptures.

The Enlightenment tradition of Baptist distinctives has inverted the order of the components. The defining distinctive has now become Christian experience as expressed in soul competency and religious freedom. From this basis, a doctrine of the church is developed that highlights and protects individual autonomy, sometimes at the expense of the corporate elements of the church. Biblical authority is interpreted in terms of individual spiritual blessings and individual Christian living as opposed to the written authority for a community of born-again believers working together for the extension of God's kingdom.

The two distinctive traditions continue to exist. Nevertheless, these two traditions also appear to be growing apart in their theological articulations. Initially, these two traditions shared similar theological assumptions and emphases. Over time, however, the two have moved further and further apart in their doctrinal positions. The Reformation tradition continues to demonstrate theological and historical continuity. The Enlightenment distinctive tradition is moving theologically further away from the Reformation tradition. The Enlightenment distinctive tradition also appears to be fragmenting within its own tradition. Later writings in this tradition share fewer theological similarities with the earlier writings identified within this tradition. For example, the Baptist distinctives writings edited by Alan Neely, *Being Baptist Means Freedom,* and Walter Shurden, *The Baptist Identity,* have little theologically in common with Baptist distinctives produced by E. Y. Mullins, George E. Horr, and James Kirtley.

In my estimation, the future prospects of each of these traditions are quite different. The Reformation tradition of Baptist distinctives contains the most historical continuity and theological stability. Based upon its history and theological stability, this tradition of Baptist distinctives will likely continue to flourish and provide a distinctive theological identity for many Baptists in the future. The Enlightenment tradition of Baptist distinctives, based upon its growing fragmentation and historical discontinuity, will either digress into theological oblivion or birth a new theological tradition for Baptist distinctives.

These divisions within Baptist distinctives illustrate two different understandings of Baptist life and Baptist theology. For example, these two distinctive traditions explain to some degree the current controversy within the Southern Baptist Convention. Those who are often described as "conservatives" tend to represent the Reformation tradition emphasis of biblical authority. "Moderates," or those who are more comfortable with some form of Christian experience as the defining distinctive, tend to represent the Enlightenment distinctive tradition. Although these two distinctive traditions cannot account for all the divisions within the controversy, they help us understand a major source of the controversy.

THE DEFINING DISTINCTIVE AND THE OTHER DISTINCTIVE COMPONENTS

Having demonstrated that there exists a "distinctive among the distinctives" (i.e., a core distinctive), I will now investigate the relationship of this core distinctive to the other distinctives. Our inquiry will hopefully answer the following questions:

Does the distinctive genre reflect a coherent interrelationship of the components, or are the components disjointed doctrinal statements? Are the distinctive components the conclusion, or the application, of the core distinctive? The structure of the discussion will follow the twofold categories of the Reformation tradition (biblical authority) and the Enlightenment tradition (Christian experience) of Baptist distinctives.

The Reformation Tradition and the Other Distinctive Components

Baptist distinctives that argue for biblical authority as the primary distinctive view the other distinctive components as the logical application of the core component. Biblical authority is the foundational premise from which the other distinctive doctrines flow. These doctrines are intentionally developed this way.

Some Baptist distinctive writings argue that the existence of Baptists and their religious practices are simply the application of their distinctive view of biblical authority. For these, Baptists are the necessary result of faithful obedience and submission to the authority of Scripture. T. T. Eaton expresses this sentiment when he says that "the fundamental principle of the Baptists is their belief in the supreme authority and absolute sufficiency of the Holy Scriptures; and their separate existence is the practical and logical result of their attempt to apply this principle in all matters of faith and practice."[15] Biblical authority for these Baptists is their most distinguishing trait and the reason for their success in the world.

As William Rone remarks, "The one fundamental principle of Baptists, and the foundation stone on which they rest as an effective Christian group in the world today, is their belief in the supreme authority and absolute sufficiency of the Holy Scriptures, especially the New Testament, as the complete and infallible guide in all matters pertaining to their faith and practice; and every other peculiarity which characterizes them is the practical outcome of this principle."[16] Baptist distinctives for these are the logical application of the core component of biblical authority.

Other treatments on Baptist distinctives apply biblical authority to the doctrine of the church. In this strand, Baptists reject all that is neither taught nor required by Scripture; thus, the Baptist understanding of the church is an extension of the Baptist understanding of biblical authority. Baptists draw "inferences for the practice of the church."

An example illustrates how this principle works. The Baptist understanding of baptism is the "search for scriptural baptism" and is considered by many the application of biblical authority. Baptists argue that believer's baptism is what is most clearly taught in the Bible; therefore, infant baptism cannot be right and must be rejected due to its lack of support from the Scriptures. Other distinctive Baptist traits that are theologically derived from biblical authority include the Baptist view of the Lord's Supper, congregational polity, and the priesthood of all believers.

Those Baptists who argue for this core component also derive soul competency from biblical authority. Based on this core component, Baptists are compelled to identify and articulate that which distinguishes them from other Christians. One of the primary doctrines identified that distinguishes Baptists from other Christians is the competency of the soul in communion with God. The concept of soul competency is perceived as such a natural outflow of biblical authority that, for some, "when one is denied or explained away, the other usually suffers like fate." The nature and authority of the Bible mandates that each person has the prerogative and responsibility to approach and deal directly with God.

THE ENLIGHTENMENT TRADITION AND THE OTHER DISTINCTIVE COMPONENTS

Another tradition of Baptist distinctives argues that Christian experience is the primary distinctive. The other distinctive components are considered the logical application of this core distinctive. Christian experience is the foundational premise from which all the other distinctives are developed.

One example of using Christian experience as the core component for interpreting the other distinctive components is Walter Rauschenbusch. He begins his discussion with the assertion that religious, or Christian, experience is the most distinctive and primary theological trait of Baptists. From this, he develops his understanding of baptism, stating that "experience is our sole requisite for receiving baptism; it is fundamental in our church life." The baptism of believers was for him the consistent application of his understanding of Christian experience. This doctrine was also determinative for Rauschenbusch's understanding of congregational polity, Christian ministry, evangelism, and the Lord's Supper.[17]

Certain expressions of Christian experience are used to develop the other distinctive components. For example, the lordship of Christ as one form of Christian experience is the "root principle" from which all other distinctive components flow. Religious freedom is used to construct other distinctive doctrines such as the authority of the Bible, the believers' church, and believer's baptism.

The most prominent expression of Christian experience as the core component is found in soul competency. This doctrine is described as "the unifying principle" for all other distinctive components. For those in this tradition, no doctrine is more fundamental to Baptists than soul competency. S. F. Skevington, for example, states that soul competency "is the principle which has shaped our [Baptist] history, dictated our attitude toward the Scriptures, formulated our conception of the Church, interpreted for us the meaning of the two New Testament ordinances, made us champions of soul [religious] liberty, sent us everywhere as missionaries of the cross, and given us a peculiar fitness to meet the spiritual needs of the age in which we are now beginning to live."[18] Maybe the best illustration of the broad, encompassing nature of soul competency as the core and shaping distinctive for Baptists is stated by Wayne Ward:

Although there is much variety of theology and practice among Baptists, certain emphases do characterize Baptists all over the United States and around the world. It is often said that Baptists have as many different viewpoints as there are Baptists—and even that quip points to the most basic characteristic of Baptist life, the religious freedom of each individual believer in his personal relationship to God. Almost all of the other Baptist distinctives flow from this basic one: their great stress upon religious liberty for all men; their rejection of any official hierarchy or bishop; their affirmation of the direct Lordship of Jesus Christ over the church congregation without any church officer to mediate it; emphasis upon a personal experience of regeneration and faith in Christ; their requirement of a personal confession of faith in Christ before baptism; and their emphasis upon a personal call of God as the basic credential for the ministry.[19]

CONCLUSION: A BAPTIST THEOLOGICAL METHOD

I want to draw several conclusions from this brief examination of Baptist distinctives. First, Baptist distinctives identify one core, determinative theological concept. This defining component is then applied logically and faithfully to shape the other distinctives. It is essential that this trend is recognized. I do not think we can appreciate or understand Baptist distinctives adequately without acknowledging this propensity. Because of this tendency, I conclude that Baptist distinctives are not simply a body of doctrine. Baptist distinctives are also a method of theology.

Second, the distinctive genre reveals both diversity and uniformity. Baptist distinctives are uniform in that they demonstrate the same method and contain essentially the same four major components previously identified. Both traditions begin with one defining component and then shape the others in light of that principle. Baptist distinctives are diverse in that they begin with two core components, biblical authority and Christian experience. This diversity is further demonstrated in the development, or the influence, of these core components upon the other distinctive components. Although sharing the same four theological components, two different starting points naturally result in two different understandings of the nature of Baptist distinctives. The other doctrines discussed in Baptist distinctives will have diverse nuances or emphases.

Finally, part of the unique theological identity of Baptists is in their consistent method of doing theology. Baptists have historically developed their distinctive theological identity within certain parameters and in certain ways. Doctrines developed outside these established parameters result in doctrinal development foreign to the Baptist identity. The "Baptist distinctive theological method" has produced a thread of doctrinal continuity found to some degree in all writings on Baptist distinctives. When deviation from the method and the components occurs, the thread of continuity is broken. The result is a loss of the theological identity unique to the Baptists.

CHAPTER THREE

A New Distinctive Tradition

I have previously noted the existence of two traditions of Baptist distinctives. The first of these is the tradition that uses biblical authority as the core component to develop the other distinctive components. The second tradition of distinctive writings uses Christian experience as the primary principle that likewise shapes the other components. The "distinctive among distinctives" for Baptists in the late nineteenth and early twentieth centuries was biblical authority. This tradition was by far the most prevalent position of the day. In the early part of the twentieth century, others began to argue for Christian experience as the interpretative distinctive.

The oldest known writing on Baptist distinctives of which I am aware that mentions religious experience as the core component is Walter Rauschenbusch's essay, "Why I Am a Baptist," published in 1905–1906. Rauschenbusch's work predates Edgar Young Mullins's *Axioms of Religion: A New Interpretation of the Baptist Faith,* published in 1908. I believe, however, Mullins's work was more influential than Rauschenbusch's monograph in the development of Christian experience as the core distinctive in Baptist life.

Two reasons explain Mullins's dominant influence. First, Rauschenbusch's writing is more personal and testimonial. Unlike Mullins, Rauschenbusch gives no reasoning or justification for his claims. He simply cites his own personal Christian experience as the basis for his development of other Baptist distinctives. Christian experience is discussed only as it pertains to his own personal spiritual pilgrimage. He does not address its implications for all Baptists. Mullins, however, provides careful argumentation for the philosophical and biblical bases for Christian experience (as expressed in soul competency). He argues for its primacy as the defining distinctive and develops the implications of his conclusions for all Baptists.

Second, others regularly appeal to Mullins's arguments as the authoritative precedent for Christian experience as the defining component. An example of the widespread appeal and popular influence of Mullins is best seen in the work of Herschel H. Hobbs, *The Axioms of Religion,* a revision of Mullins's earlier work.[1] Rauschenbusch's work does not appear to be recognized by others or to have exerted any influence apart from himself. I am aware of no one who argues for Christian experience as the interpretative component who appeals to Rauschenbusch as an authoritative source. For these reasons, I consider Mullins's work the point when the paradigm for Baptist distinctives shifted.

As previously noted, the first major treatise to argue for a redefining of the primary distinctive of Baptists was *The*

Axioms of Religion: A New Interpretation of the Baptist Faith. As the title suggests, Mullins was quite intentional in proposing a new standard for the distinctive genre. He elevated the volitional component (I will use "Christian experience" and "volitional component" interchangeably) to a level of authority that had previously been reserved for biblical authority. This is not to say that Christian experience was not discussed within the distinctive genre, for it certainly was present within the volitional component. Mullins rather infused into the genre a new interpretative distinctive. *The Axioms of Religion* was a momentous shift in the prevailing understanding of the theological distinctives of Baptists. It birthed a second distinctive tradition from which Baptists would elaborate their unique theological identity.

Because of the prominent place he has in the history and development of Baptist distinctives, Mullins's impact upon Baptist distinctives merits our attention. I want to touch briefly upon the philosophical influences that may have shaped his thought, examine the way in which he developed his theology, investigate his understanding of Christian experience, and then develop the significance of Mullins for Baptist distinctives.

The technical discussion of this chapter may intimidate some readers. And, theoretically, one could forego reading this section and still benefit overall from this study. I believe, however, that readers will broaden their understanding of Baptist distinctives if they will diligently work through this material. By understanding Mullins and his influence on Baptist distinctives, one can gain a better appreciation of the Baptist distinctive genre and have a better grasp on the status of contemporary Baptists and their distinctive theology.

PHILOSOPHICAL INFLUENCES

Mullins's theological method and its implications for Baptist distinctives can only be understood in light of the influences that shaped his thought. Identifying these influences, however, is easier said than done. For one thing, various opinions exist regarding the persons and movements that directed his thought. For another, Mullins, as was common in his time, did not carefully document his sources when writing. Due to the scarcity of citations, influences upon Mullins are difficult to determine. Several shaping factors on his thought can, however, be identified. These include the pragmatism of William James, the experientialism of F. D. E. Schleiermacher, and the personalism of Borden Parker Bowne. Mullins sought those philosophies which were experientially based, believing them to be of "the highest degree" and quite favorable to the construction of theology.

WILLIAM JAMES AND PRAGMATISM

Of all the influence upon Mullins's thought, the impact of William James and pragmatism is the most easily discerned. Mullins himself openly admits James's influence. William James is considered one of the major formulators of a philosophical movement called pragmatism. Pragmatism is basically the idea that the meaning or truth of any proposition is found in its practical effects.

Mullins found pragmatism attractive because it rejected abstract, highly rationalistic explanations of reality. Materialistic principles of cause and effect were for Mullins inadequate to explain life and the universe. Pragmatism allowed the human will to enter into the process of obtaining knowledge. Real knowledge came from the actual experiences of life. For Mullins, real truth was that which is "workable in our life-experiences." In other words, humans apprehend truth as they encounter, or experience, reality with the totality of their beings.

Pragmatism was for Mullins more than a philosophical interpretation of reality. It was the means to discover truth. Mullins considered James's understanding of truth and experience as the common denominator among all religions, including Christianity. Mullins did, however, move beyond James by emphasizing that Jesus Christ was the direction and culmination of Christian experience.[2]

Mullins leaned heavily upon pragmatism, especially when he developed his own epistemology, his theory of knowing. He perceived pragmatism as the best explanation for discovering truth. As such, "truth" was only "true" to the extent that it could be applied relevantly in human experience.

F. D. E. SCHLEIERMACHER

F. D. E. Schleiermacher was another influence in Mullins's thought. Although sympathetic to some of Schleiermacher's system of thought, Mullins also found much in his system objectionable. For example, he described Schleiermacher's definition of religion, a "feeling of absolute dependence," as inadequate. Further, Mullins believed Schleiermacher was in error when the latter elevated this feeling of absolute dependence to the highest ideal in religion. Mullins also believed (rightfully so) that Schleiermacher's philosophy supported and promoted pantheism (i.e., the belief that God is all and all is God) and not Christianity. For Mullins, Christ was not a mere example of religious experience (as taught by Schleiermacher) but rather the author and object of the religious experience.

What Mullins did find useful in Schleiermacher's system was the role that human experience played in developing theology. Human experience has its own independent value in the theological task. Mullins believed Schleiermacher was right when he said that one's experience of Christ has the same level of authenticity as any other experience in life or, for that matter, any other reality in existence. As such, religious experience merits the same credible recognition and source for theology as any other religious discipline or philosophy. Mullins incorporated the idea of the objective worth of "experiencing the infinite" into his thought. He further seemed comfortable with Schleiermacher's definition of the consciousness of sin as a feeling of dependence. Christian redemption for Mullins was a deliverance from this state of moral helplessness.[3]

BORDEN PARKER BOWNE AND PERSONALISM

Borden Parker Bowne's development of personalism may well be the most prominent philosophical influence upon Mullins's thought. Personalism, or personal idealism, is a philosophy that perceives ultimate reality as persons or selves. Mullins found Bowne's emphases quite helpful in defending and presenting the Christian religion.

Mullins believed personalism, with its emphasis upon reality as persons, truer to the facts of experience. Personalism recognizes the elements of will, feelings, and intellect. All that people are and all of the reality that they know are apprehended through these elements. These dynamics of human existence present "man in the totality of his relations, to nature, to other persons in human society, and to God." Personalism asserts that "ultimate reality is a Person; that we as the creation of his hands are true persons; that we are endowed with freedom; that the goal of history is a perfect society of men and women in fellowship with God."

Mullins found this philosophical perspective attractive because it upheld personality as the only type of entity through which the world could be completely comprehended. Beginning with the conviction that ultimate reality was a person, Mullins asserted that man, created by that person, was a personal being. As such, man was endowed with freedom while living under the providential plan of the divine person. Mullins had a strong affinity for a system that recognized the universe as one of relations between persons, not of things or blind forces. Personalism emphasized man's knowledge and freedom. Knowledge was that which was derived from communication with another, i.e., God, and freedom was God's reflection in man, who was made in his image.

Personalism also placed the concept of causation with God, who for Mullins was the moving and efficient cause of all things. Mullins's affinity to personalism probably was due in part to the idea that personalism "preserves the Christian values." Knowledge of God was obtained through the experience of the human person relating to the divine person.[4]

CONCLUSION

These philosophical conceptions allowed Mullins to construct his epistemology upon six fundamental assumptions. These assumptions undergird all his thought regarding life and religion (particularly Christianity). They are particularly relevant in Mullins's assertion that Christian experience is the defining distinctive and his experiential interpretation of the other core components.

The first premise is that reality ultimately exists external to and independent of humanity. In other words, Mullins perceived ultimate reality as the triune God of the Christian faith. This God is separate in existence and being from humanity. Second, God brings structure and order to the universe. The world in which human beings exist has unity and meaning, found ultimately in the person of God. The world cannot be fully and completely known apart from God. Third, parts of the physical and spiritual realms of the universe cohere. Physical beings are also spiritual beings. As such, they have the capacity to know and relate to God.

Fourth, the human faculties of reason and emotion provide true knowledge of objective reality. These aspects of human nature supply reliable information about the universe. Fifth, human beings discover truth as their entire being is involved in the processes of life. Mullins understood involvement in life as the human experience of persons relating to the world of nature, to other human beings in society, and ultimately to the person of God. Finally, human personality is endowed with the capacity to act upon and be acted upon by natural objects and can distinguish itself from and interact with other humans.[5]

These premises are for Mullins facts to be accepted, not theories to be proved. These assumptions are among the "simplest and most fundamental postulates" of all human thought. They are true for all people and form the very idea of truth. And they would in part form the basis on which Mullins would construct his understanding of Baptist distinctives.

MULLINS AND CHRISTIAN EXPERIENCE

For Mullins, experience provides true knowledge for the Christian faith and supplies Christian belief with theological content. He defines Christian experience as "the state or condition produced in the mental, moral and spiritual nature of man when he conforms to the conditions which Christianity declares to be necessary to union and fellowship with God."[6] He further notes that "the revelation of God in Christ possesses all the elements which are required to establish its truth. It is known as an objective fact. It is then known in its results in the subjective experience."[7]

Mullins argues that Christian experience encompasses the entire Christian life. For him, Christian experience is the totality of experiences that become a person's through fellowship with God in Christ. This experience not only includes the beginning, conversion, but also includes all the benefits and realities of regeneration. This experience is a corporate experience as well as an individual experience. It includes all that properly belongs to the experience in the community of Christians, the past as well as the present. Christian experience includes certain essential elements, but these elements appear in endless variations among particular individuals.

Christian experience is a relational engagement, or "transaction," between God as person and the individual as person. God takes the initiative in the experience, encountering persons in the message of salvation by grace in Christ. Upon the free, uncoerced reception of the gospel, the individual experiences conversion, a term that Mullins uses to encompass redemption, forgiveness, repentance, etc. The experience of the Christian is characterized by an "inner connectedness, the mutual dependence, and the moral and spiritual completeness" of all aspects of conversion. Human beings are created in God's image and have the capacity for knowledge and communion with God. This capacity makes possible a new creation in regeneration as God renews "the image which has been marred by sin." God's renewing brings forgiveness and justification.

Knowledge arises in Christian experience in the same manner in which it arises from other experiences. The foundational principles of the reception and appropriation of knowledge are the same in all realms. Realities are presented in experience. Knowledge thus arises from the facts received through the experience. The knowledge is "not merely 'information about' those realities, but 'acquaintance with' them." Christian knowledge arises from the personal interaction of God's person with the person of the individual in Christ. The information from this experience is gradually synthesized and constructed into a doctrinal system. The Christian experience alone is inadequate for theological formation. The guidance of the New Testament is required.

Although conceding that the New Testament is significant for guidance in the experience, Mullins stipulates that the experience must precede the individual's encounter with the Scriptures. It is "through his experience that the Christian acquires a vital relation to the New Testament which enables him to understand it."[8]

Based upon this understanding, Christian experience produces "a distinct order of facts, a system of moral and spiritual forces, whose laws may be traced and systematically set forth." The experience reveals "a group of spiritual causes which produce their proper effects in human consciousness and in man's moral and spiritual activities." This activity results in the development of interpretative doctrines. The theologian must remain connected to the experience in order to avoid an abstract analysis of the facts of review through the experience.

MULLINS'S THEOLOGICAL METHOD

Christian theology for Mullins is the "systematic and scientific explanation" of the order of facts that arise from the experiential relationship between God and man. These facts are of two types: facts of experience and facts of God's historical revelation in Jesus Christ. With regard to Baptists, Mullins considers them the most consistent and complete expression of this definition of Christian theology.

Drawing upon Bowne's personalism, James's pragmatism, and Schleiermacher's experientialism, Mullins developed a theological method that produced doctrine from experience. He believed that the doctrines of Christianity gave prominence to Christian experience. It was the method he adopted in his theological method and construction of Baptist distinctives.

Mullins perceives Christianity as a religion of experience, and Christian theology is that which analyzes and interprets this religion. Subjectivism is not the final arbiter of truth and authority in this religion of experience. His experiential method rather attempts to combine several factors that Mullins considers as sources of theology. The basic premise is that Jesus Christ is God's historical revelation to humanity. The New Testament is the "indispensable source" of knowledge about the historical revelation of God in Christ and his work of salvation. The Holy Spirit works and guides individuals to accept Christ. It is in and through the Holy Spirit that the meaning of Christian facts are "brought home" to persons. Christians must define and understand their spiritual experiences as God's Holy Spirit reveals Christ to them.

Mullins offers several advantages of his experiential method. It avoids the excess speculation and exaggerated intellectualism by grounding theology on the facts supplied through experience. In doing so, experience becomes the focal point for theology and the means by which theological claims are verified. The experiential method also provides the factual basis for the presentation of Christian truths in a logical manner. It answers the question, Who is Jesus Christ and how is he related to my experience of God's redeeming grace? Further, the experiential method provides the surest foundation for theology by interweaving the facts of history and experience together. The experience of God in Christ provides the perspective from which other religious evidences are rightly evaluated. Mullins asserts that experience provides the most certain knowledge of God. The experiential method thus expresses the Christian faith in such a way as to demonstrate that human autonomy and human freedom are characteristic of Christianity.[9]

Of significance for writings on Baptist distinctives is Mullins's final point. The experiential method also defines the nature of the Bible's authority. Biblical skeptics often argue that the Bible cannot be an authoritative and infallible guide in religion because of the supposed existence of historical, scientific, and literary errors. In response to this objection, Mullins suggests that the inner, subjective authority of the Christian's experience of God's redeeming grace in Christ corresponds to the authority of the outer, objective authority of the record of God's revelation in Christ. The Christian's experience provides the proper perspective from which to see and understand the Bible.

Mullins infused religious experience into his understanding of religious authority. He asserts the importance of God's objective revelation in the historic person of Jesus Christ. He attempts to protect the objective nature of this authoritative act of God. He argues that this objective revelation is appropriated by the experiential working of the Holy Spirit within the hearts of man. The Scriptures are rightly understood only within the context of Christian experience.

Mullins at times appears to argue that Christian experience is that which infuses the Bible with its authority. The objectivity of God's historical revelation is established and verified through Christian experience. Christian experience for Mullins is the element that verifies and interprets truth. Further, experience is the condition in which God's truth is known and appropriated. In a sense, Mullins could be construed as saying that revelation is only objective within the context of a subjective experience.

Mullins argues on occasion for the Scriptures as authoritative over religious experience. On other occasions, religious experience becomes the channel for the authority of the Bible. Still at other times, he so emphasizes the authoritative nature of religious experience that he subordinates the authority of the Bible to the authority of experience. With regard to Baptist distinctives, Mullins inadvertently implies that Christian experience is either equal to or above the historical revelation of Jesus Christ as recorded in the New Testament.

This is illustrated in Mullins's statement that "knowledge of God becomes ours then in a threefold way: First from the original source, Jesus Christ; secondly, through the authoritative record, the New Testament; and thirdly, through the experience of God's grace in Christ, wrought in us by the Holy Spirit. We can only understand Christ and the Bible through the experience of God's saving grace."[10]

Unlike his predecessors who used Scripture in their polemics against non-Baptist Christian practices, Mullins uses religious experience to identify and critique the ecclesiological practices of other Christian denominations.[11] Non-Baptist Christians and other religions are deemed deficient in light of the Baptist emphasis on a personal experience with the living God through Jesus Christ. The use of Christian experience as opposed to Scripture as the polemical component is a shift from previous Baptist practices and illustrates the high degree of importance Mullins placed upon the authoritative nature of experience.

MULLINS'S SIGNIFICANCE FOR BAPTIST DISTINCTIVES

Mullins sought to develop a theology that would communicate the Christian faith in his day in vibrant fashion. He modified and combined features of pragmatism, experientialism, and personalism so that the result was a theological method that emphasized Christian experience. Real knowledge was imparted through the Christian experience. This knowledge not only emphasized "information about" but also "acquaintance with" the highest reality: the revelation of God in Jesus Christ. As God encountered the believer in the individual's experience, the believer was given an unhindered and undistorted view of reality. The believer came to know God through his experience as a person who is active in his life, transforming the entirety of the human's personality. A person was enabled through his experience to see accurately God's historical revelation.

Mullins carried his theological method into his construction of Baptist distinctives. His strong emphasis on experience as a source for theology introduced new inroads of theological methodology in Baptist life and the distinctive genre. Mullins himself asserted that "we have introduced an innovation in general discussions of Christian evidences and have employed Christian experience as an important evidence of Christianity."[12] He contended that Christians are entitled to the belief that their experience of Christ is a factual source for knowledge and theology. Mullins concluded that Christian experience formed the ultimate basis for a worldview for all other facts of experience in the personal and physical realms.

Mullins elevated within the distinctive genre of Baptists the role of Christian experience as a means of defining and obtaining the factual evidence or testimony for the Christian religion. Mullins sought diligently to adhere to the notion that doctrinal development should occur through Christian experience only when Christian experience works in tandem with and in subordination to the revelation of Jesus Christ in the Bible and the guidance of the Holy Spirit. Despite his best efforts, Mullins inadvertently placed greater weight on experience than the Scriptures, thereby giving Christian experience a new status within Baptist distinctive genre. Christian experience became a new interpretative distinctive for the formulation of the other Baptist distinctives. The individual, as an autonomous being, was now the focal point for developing and interpreting Baptist distinctives.

CHAPTER FOUR

A Distinctive Authority

In previous chapters I addressed the theoretical issues regarding Baptist distinctives. I defined which writings should be considered treatments on Baptist distinctives and which ones should not. I argued that this kind of literature constituted a definite theological genre, a Baptist distinctive genre. This genre provided a confessional theology for Baptists. Part of my analysis also touched upon the way Baptists developed their unique doctrines. A core, interpretative component is used to construct and interpret the other distinctive components.

I now want to consider the topic of content. What exactly are the theological concepts found in this genre? I alluded to some of the doctrines in earlier discussions, particularly in the section on the components of Baptist distinctives and the discussion on the interpretative distinctive. I wish to explore in more detail the doctrinal content of Baptist distinctives.

At this point, a few words of procedure are in order. In the following chapters, I will examine theological ideas found within Baptist distinctives. I will present these under the categories of the Reformation tradition and the Enlightenment tradition of Baptist distinctives. I believe that this kind of examination helps in comparing and contrasting the various emphases contained in these writings. My intention is to survey a sampling of materials within each major tradition. Space restricts the amount of information and the number of persons I will cover. I have selected those writings on Baptist distinctives that either develop unique doctrinal themes or depict the views of major figures in Baptist life.

Some may find this approach unappealing. The survey and examination of actual writings on Baptist distinctives could appear a bit tedious and pedantic. Yet, this approach is in part one of the major reasons I developed this work. Many opinions are offered on the exact nature of what are and what are not Baptist distinctives. The method I am using surveys and summarizes what the distinctive writings actually say. I want the writings and authors to speak for themselves. This approach brings a measure of objectivity into what has classically been a very subjective, opinionated discussion. Further, this approach provides a broad theological overview that emphasizes the unique contributions of each document examined. I trust my choices will highlight the interesting perspectives of select writings while also representing the ideas of all the treatises in each distinctive tradition.

Each of the following chapters will examine one of the distinctive components with the exception of the polemical. Because polemical intention is contained within the formulation of the other components, I will not devote a chapter exclusively to it. Readers will see this component woven within discussions of other issues. Polemical intention is most clearly visible in the discussions of the ecclesiological component.

The following chapter examines the epistemological component. Epistemology addresses the basis of knowledge: the theory of knowing. Of particular relevance for the current discussion is the way that Baptist distinctive writings construct their foundation for religious knowledge. The Reformation tradition asserts that the Bible is the beginning point for religious knowledge. The Enlightenment tradition argues that religious experience is the foundational premise for religious knowledge. All Baptist distinctive writings discuss in some measure the Bible and Christian experience. The issue before us is: How do Baptist distinctives relate these two concepts? Is the Bible an objective authority apart from an individual religious experience? Is an experience of God necessary before the Bible gains religious authority? Is religious authority some kind of mutual relationship between individual experience and biblical authority?

RELIGIOUS AUTHORITY IN THE REFORMATION TRADITION OF BAPTIST DISTINCTIVES

Baptists in this tradition have always viewed their origin and existence in relation to the prominent place the Bible has enjoyed in their theological expression. Baptists do not adhere to a belief of biblical inspiration that differs from other Christian denominations. In other words, there is not a distinctively Baptist view of how the Bible came to be or the nature of the Bible's authority. Baptists rather argue that their view of religious authority, their epistemology, is different from non-Baptist Christians. As I noted previously, Baptists insist that their consistent and exclusive adherence to the Scriptures for matters of faith distinguishes them from other Christians. Baptists believe that other Christian denominations elevate certain religious traditions to the same level as the Bible. Baptists argue that any theological perspective or tradition that does not have clear or strong biblical support must be rejected.

Two expressions of religious authority exist within the Reformation tradition. Some Baptists assert the authority of the Bible in general terms. In other words, this group does not necessarily distinguish between the authority of Old and New Testaments. Other Baptists narrow religious authority primarily to the New Testament. This group does affirm that the entire Bible is the inspired and authoritative revelation from God. They also believe that both testaments are of value for knowing and relating to God. Yet, for reasons soon revealed, these Baptists focus upon the New Testament as the supreme authority for faith and practice.

THE ENTIRE BIBLE

The relation between Baptists and the Protestant Reformers is one of the early themes addressed in distinctive genre. In particular, select authors of distinctive writings view Baptists as the logical outcome to the Protestant Reformation principle of *sola Scriptura*. *Sola Scriptura* is the idea that the Scriptures or the Bible alone is the only authority for Christian faith and practice. This group of distinctive writings contends that the Bible as the sole religious authority is best seen in Baptists.

Two examples will illustrate this point. In his argument for Baptists as the only true religious reformers, John Quincy Adams states that the feature that differentiates Baptists from all other Christian denominations is the entire Word of God as the sole and final source of religious authority. True reformation occurs only through a Christian people who build their faith and practice exclusively upon the Bible. According to Adams,

Baptists are the only people who meet this criterion. He suggested that this thoroughgoing commitment to the Bible is what would bring a "complete and thorough reform" of the church and society. This perspective of the Bible's authority would in turn result in the existence of the primitive, or New Testament, church. The presence and ministry of the primitive church would "achieve a complete and entire Reformation" of the world. This restoration would occur only when the sole authority of God's Word was implemented in all realms. Restoring the true, New Testament church is the mission of Baptists.[1]

Other Baptists also see themselves as the truest expression of the Reformation tenet of "the Bible alone." *Baptist Why and Why Not* concedes that all Christians are similar in their general acceptance of the Bible as the Word of God. What Baptists believe about the nature and the teachings of the Bible, however, is the distinguishing feature between them and other Christian denominations. This work asserts that "we [Baptists] accept the Scriptures as an all-sufficient and infallible rule of faith and practice, and insist upon the absolute inerrancy and sole authority of the Word of God." Further, "the fundamental principle of the Baptists is their belief in the supreme authority and absolute sufficiency of the Holy Scriptures; and their separate existence is the practical and logical result of their attempt to apply this principle in all matters of religion."[2] This "separate existence" is the logical conclusion to *sola Scriptura* and distinguishes Baptists from the other Reformers.

The following quotation exemplifies the sentiment of those who support the idea of the Bible alone as religious authority. Although lengthy, it provides an excellent illustration of the conviction of those in this tradition.

And let me show you how it is that this fundamental principle has led to the separate existence of the

Baptists and to the peculiarities that mark their
denominational life. . . . Take for example, the question of baptism. Luther said that the primitive baptism was immersion and that the primitive practice
should be restored. The Baptists said the same thing
and following out of their belief immersed all who
came to them even though they had been sprinkled
before. Strange to say, for this Luther hated the
Baptists hardly less than he hated the Catholics.
Calvin said that the word *baptize* means to immerse
and that it is certain that immersion was the practice
of the primitive churches, but that in this matter the
churches ought to have liberty. Here now are the
points of agreement and the points of difference
between the Reformers on the one hand and the
Baptists on the other. They all agreed that immersion
was the practice of the primitive churches. Luther and
Calvin thought that they were at liberty to practice
another form, the Baptists said that we ought to do
what the Master commands; and that we have no liberty to change a positive ordinance which he has
ordained. Here the work of separation begins. The
issue was not as to what the act of baptism is, but
whether we have the right to change it. Before the
court of the highest scholarship of the world it has
never been an open question as to what the true baptism is. It really is not now, as it was not in the time
of Luther and Calvin. The question is about the right
to change it; and it is not that Baptists think too much
of one form above another. I am frank to say for
myself, that if it were a matter left to our choice
whether we should immerse or sprinkle, while immersion is a beautiful and significant ordinance and

sprinkling is a meaningless ceremony, still I would give up immersion rather than divide Christendom on a mere rite:—I say if it were left to our choice. But it has never been left to our choice: And when others say that they will change the ordinance, the question between them and us is, not what is the true baptism but whether there is any right or authority to change it. Baptists do not yield their position about baptism because it is the surface indication of a great underlying principle. Principles are of use to us because of the guidance they afford us in practical life. What honor or consistency is there in avowing a principle and then denying it in our daily conduct? We see how it is then that the peculiarity of Baptists upon immersion results from their fundamental position. They must be peculiar or they must give up the principle that the Word of God is our supreme and all-sufficient rule.[3]

Some Baptists perceive that "the Bible alone" emphasis distinctly separates (maybe even isolates) Baptists from other Christian denominations. Baptists justify their existence and denominational life because of the consistent application of this concept. J. M. Pendleton acknowledges a shared consensus with non-Baptist Christians regarding the recognition of the Bible "as the supreme standard of faith and practice." For Pendleton, the Baptist view of the Bible's authority categorically distinguishes them from other Christians. Baptists depart theologically from other Christians with an adamant contention for the sole place of the Scriptures for Christian belief and practice. This principle differentiates Baptists "from Presbyterians, Episcopalians, Congregationalists, Lutherans, Methodists." The consistent application of this concept in church life justifies their denominational existence.[4]

Some Baptists assert that the unmediated acceptance of the Bible's exclusive authority results in Baptist churches. J. B. Gambrell contends that the Scriptures as a religious guide is "a cardinal principle with Baptists." For him, biblical authority eliminates the authority of councils, popes, synods, conferences, bishops, etc. This view of the Bible "gives no place" to religious tradition "as a supplement to the teaching of the Bible." Baptists believe what they do about baptism, the Lord's Supper, and church polity because these are fixed "in nature and order" in the Bible.[5]

The sufficient and unchanging authority of the Bible is the emphasis developed by W. R. White. The written "Word of God," according to White, provides unwavering guidance for the people of God in their doctrinal beliefs and practical ministries. The Bible is offered as the only sufficient "authoritative criterion." The Scriptures are unchanging in that they are the divine revelation of an unchanging God. The timeless nature of the biblical text is always relevant. Scripture's authority and teachings address the spiritual life and concerns of all persons in all times and places. Baptists claim that "the guiding principle for the solution of all disputed issues in the realm of faith and practice" is found in the Bible. Traditions, councils, and synods cannot provide the sufficiency and stable authority of the Scripture. The Bible is absolute in the "quality" and "certainty" of its teaching.[6]

The Bible's exclusive authority, according to Jack Hoad, promotes a "spirit of nonconformity" among Baptists. Baptists are nonconformists in that they adhere to the Bible as their sole authority for faith and practice. Baptists insist that Christians are to be "ruled absolutely by the Holy Scriptures," both in their churches and in their personal lives. "The Word of God remains an unchanging standard which is not modified by the times and situations. All traditions and rites, not possessing an explicit base, are not required of him." By conforming themselves exclusively to the Bible's authority, Baptists become secular nonconformists.

Interestingly, Hoad regards non-Baptist Christians also as nonconformists, but in a different manner. Other Christians are nonconformists because they submit themselves to "religious institutions" not found in the Bible and usually at odds with biblical teaching. These Christians do not conform absolutely to the Scriptures. For Hoad, one cannot understand Baptists without appreciating their view of the Bible as their exclusive religious authority.[7]

THE NEW TESTAMENT

Some Baptists argue for the exclusive authority of the New Testament. John Broadus suggests that both Old and New Testaments are the revelation of God and are therefore authoritative for God's people. He qualifies this, however, by noting that Baptists, as New Testament believers, distinguish themselves theologically from other Christian denominations by constructing their belief and practice upon the New Testament. Christian institutions rest upon the direct teachings of the New Testament.[8] P. Lovene, who also adopts this line of reasoning, contends that the application of Old Testament laws to New Testament Christians results in deviant and harmful doctrines:

> The teachings of Christ and His apostles must be the rule of life and teaching for His followers. . . . But right here may I state as my firm conviction, that applying Old Testament laws to New Testament times is one of the most fruitful sources of such dark blotches as have marred the record of many professed followers of Christ. This perilous course the Baptists have seen and avoided.[9]

Lovene points to doctrines such as infant baptism, a special priesthood, and state churches as examples of harmful doctrines.

B. H. Carroll also advocates the New Testament as the authority for religious practice. He affirms that the Old Testament is inspired by God and is profitable for spiritual lessons. The authority of the Old Testament, however, is encapsulated and fulfilled in the New Testament. Carroll states that the Old Testament, as a "typical, educational, and transitory system," is fulfilled by Christ. Christ "nailed" the Old Testament to the cross, so that "as a standard of law and a way of life" it is "taken out of the way." Christians should no longer go to the Old Testament to find Christian law or Christian institutions because the New Testament has now become the "law" for them.

Carroll strongly emphasizes this point when he expounds that "the New Testament is the law of Christianity. All the New Testament is the law of Christianity. The New Testament is all the law of Christianity. The New Testament always will be all the law of Christianity." This assertion is the point of departure of Baptists from other Protestants. He notes that "Romanists" and "Protestants" alike affirm the notion that "the Bible alone" is the religion of Christianity. Carroll believes, however, that "when Baptists say that the New Testament is the only law for Christian institutions they part company, if not theoretically at least practically, with most of the Protestant world, as well as from the Greeks and Romanists" (notice the polemical intention in Carroll's remarks about non-Baptist groups).[10]

The emphasis of the authority of the New Testament was for some Baptists reason not to affiliate formally with certain religious groups. Henry Cook affirms such a position. He argues against Baptists, particularly Southern Baptists, officially joining the National and World Councils of Churches.

The rationale for his arguments to remain separate is the authority of the New Testament as the basis for all Baptist beliefs. The New Testament regulates Baptist convictions and conduct. The authority of the New Testament is the fundamental position from which Baptists begin and "from it they draw all their conclusions." All of Baptist life is influenced and developed from this concept.

Cook states that Baptists are united in the conviction that the ultimate standard is the New Testament. Baptists always start with the supreme authority of the New Testament, and they attempt to deal with every issue of doctrine and conduct from this position. Cook was concerned that Baptists, by affiliating with these interdenominational groups, would eventually be tempted to compromise and ultimately relinquish their distinctive religious authority.[11]

Robert A. Baker supports the dual emphasis of the Old Testament finding fulfillment in the New Testament and the unmediated authority of the New Testament. He suggests that the New Testament, "without traditions, without church councils, without ecclesiastical sanction," is the sole authority and the essential distinctive of Baptists. It is the "pre-eminent" standard for New Testament Christians. The ultimate test for any teaching in Christianity is not its agreement with human patterns but with the New Testament. Christ's authority is found in the New Testament. The Old Testament's promises were fulfilled in the Son of God, "whose majestic person swallowed up all ceremonial law; whose authoritative words, 'but I say unto you,' put new meaning into moral law; and who, as both Builder and Foundation, established his church in history." The effort to conform to the principles of Jesus as contained within the New Testament is the ongoing Baptist quest.

Baker further suggests that wherever the Bible has been read and followed throughout the centuries, "New Testament

Christians" have existed. Baptists claim a "spiritual kinship" with these Christians; in this sense these groups are "baptistic." Baptists oppose those who alter or eliminate the specific teachings of the New Testament and those who equate the authority of the New Testament with religious traditions. Baptists instead "believe that the effort of Christians today should be directed, not toward modifying, but toward reproducing the pattern of the New Testament." Baptists can only claim to be "Baptist" to the extent that they unequivocally adhere to this essential doctrine.[12]

Winthrop S. Hudson states that the New Testament is "not a law book." Minute regulations for all of life's contingencies will not be found there. The "phenomenon" of seeking "detailed regulations" is a departure "from the precise prescriptions by which the life of Israel was ordered under the Old Covenant." Baptists should instead derive general theological principles from the biblical text. From these principles Baptists draw "inferences for the practice of the church." Baptists believe that much of the organization and practice of contemporary church life deviates significantly from the biblical model, often distorting or misrepresenting the gospel. The exclusive reliance upon the New Testament for faith and practice is the only safeguard that keeps basic Christian convictions from deviation.[13]

RELIGIOUS AUTHORITY IN THE ENLIGHTENMENT TRADITION

I will now examine religious authority in the Enlightenment tradition of Baptist distinctives. As was the case with the Reformation strand, this tradition has a variety of unique expressions. In the first section I will analyze those Baptist distinctive writings that understand religious authority as a combination of Christian experience and the Bible. In the second section I will investigate another group of Baptist distinctives that understands religious authority as the lordship of Christ and the Bible.

RELIGIOUS AUTHORITY: CHRISTIAN EXPERIENCE AND THE BIBLE

E. Y. Mullins gives an important role to the Bible in his overall paradigm of religious authority. He does this by linking biblical authority with his understanding of religious experience. Christ, as the medium of God's revelation, takes theoretical ideas about God and makes them understandable to the believer through religious experience. When the believer experiences God in the context of a personal encounter, that is the point when Scripture truly gains its authoritative value. The essence of the Bible's authority is therefore experientially derived. For Mullins, this perspective of religious authority is a dynamic understanding and has both an objective and a subjective element.

Religious authority is objective because the Bible is an anchor that keeps the believer connected to the Christ of history. Religious authority is subjective in that Christian experience is the medium through which the soul encounters and submits to the personal authority of Christ. The Bible becomes the "rule of faith and practice" when the Spirit, who interprets it to the church and guides the church in obedience, illuminates it.[14]

For H. Wheeler Robinson, religious authority is found in the shared religious experiences of the individual with those preserved in the Scriptures. Robinson suggests that Baptists, like other Protestant Christians, appeal to the Bible to justify their beliefs and practices. Yet, unlike these other Christians, Baptists have a distinctive understanding of the Bible in their view of religious authority. Individual religious experience is characteristic of the Baptist faith and distinctly separates Baptists from other Christian groups.

For Robinson, the Bible is more than merely a book of precepts or laws for the life of faith. Its authority does not reside in its ability to issue commandments. Rather, Scripture's authority is found in the record of human, religious experiences contained within it. He disparages the practice of citing biblical texts as an "authoritative precedent." The believer should not appeal to the Bible as a textbook of Christian teachings but rather as a "source-book" of common religious experiences. Robinson does not view his understanding of religious authority as mere subjectivism. Rather, "to have the New Testament in one's hand, as a necessary consequence of one's denominational testimony, is the great safeguard against unscriptural teaching, the surest foundation for a faith that claims to continue the principles of the Reformation."

Further, the "constant appeal to Scripture for the distinctive denominational testimony, which is found with what many will think wearisome iteration, has had an important result. It has helped to make and keep Baptists a Bible-loving Church." The Bible therefore serves to regulate and interpret the person's experience of God.[15]

Walter Rauschenbusch subordinates the authority of the Bible to religious experience. His understanding of Christianity and authority begins with religious experience, which for him was the essence of Baptist thought and ministry. In fact, the Christian faith as believed by Baptists sets "spiritual experience boldly to the front as the one great thing in religion. . . . Experience is our sole requisite" for a life of faith.

Rauschenbusch rejects the prevalent understanding of the biblical authority tradition and instead argues that the Bible's authority is derived from religious experience. He suggests that the distinctive contribution of Baptists is not the affirmation of a "Bible as a creed" but rather the Bible as a history of the religious experiences of others. He rejects the notion that the intent of the Bible is to provide objective teachings that shape faith and practice. The Scriptures are rather a record of "what holy men have believed," a "religious history" that models the "purest and freshest form of Christianity"—that is, the self-evidencing power of God's living word authenticated by God's Spirit in the heart of the believer.

Rauschenbusch calls upon Baptists to move beyond their traditional views of biblical authority and to allow religious experience to impart new life and awaken new thought. Christian experience, as preserved and interpreted by the Bible, is what Rauschenbusch believed to be the distinctive Baptist view of religious authority.[16]

George E. Horr states that the authority of the Scriptures is derived from religious experience. He suggests that religious authority resides in the "response of the human soul to the revelation of God in Christ." Horr does not believe that religious authority is objectively found in the Bible. Instead, he asserts that religious authority is an inward work of the Holy Spirit which bears witness to God's Word upon the hearts of men. Scripture is authoritative only when validated by the internal witness of the Holy Spirit within the believer. Doctrines of inspiration and other objective understandings are insufficient means of explaining the religious authority of the Bible.[17]

Cecil Sherman contends that the absolute competency of the individual is the epistemological basis for Baptists. Although he does "recognize the supreme worth of the Bible and the New Testament in particular for Baptist churches," Sherman subordinates the authoritative role of the Bible to the "competence of the individual to interpret the Bible." He suggests that Baptist authority is a "loose" authority and is intentionally "designed to stay that way" by God. The confidence for religious authority resides in the right of private interpretation of each individual. The "way of Jesus" is inherent in this principle.

Sherman therefore argues that Baptists should advocate a religious authority that is expressed in the freedom of the individual to interpret the nature and the doctrine of the Scriptures for themselves. "The right of private interpretation of the Bible is so basic to 'being Baptist' until any diminishing of this right, any erosion of the principle is straying from 'being Baptist.'"[18]

RELIGIOUS AUTHORITY AS THE LORDSHIP OF CHRIST

Some Baptists locate religious authority in the direct, unmediated lordship of Christ over the believer. John D. Freeman defines the "essential Baptist principle" as "an acute awareness and vivid consciousness of the sovereignty of Christ, accompanied by a steadfast determination to secure the complete and consistent recognition of His personal, direct and undelegated authority over the souls of men." The lordship of Christ involves a union of Christ's "personal saviourhood and sovereignty" apprehended within the context of Christian experience. Freeman suggests that the experiential authority of Christ's lordship is "one in Christ" with the authority of the New Testament. The Christian experience of Christ's lordship establishes and justifies the authority of the New Testament. The New Testament in turn shapes and guides the experiential authority of Christ's lordship in the individual Christian.[19]

Wayne Ward proposes that the authority of the Bible is an authority derived from a religious experience expressed through the lordship of Christ. The Bible's authority is encapsulated within the lordship of Christ and expressed within the dynamic of Christian experience. Baptists are bound to submit to the Scriptures because Christ's lordship is defined within the Bible. For Ward, Baptists believe that Christ rules his church and that his lordship is exercised through the "inner witness of the Holy Spirit" and the "written word." The reason that Baptists accept the Bible's written authority is because of their prior conception of Christ's living authority. The written authority of the Bible is derived from the experiential authority of Christ's lordship.[20]

Certain Baptists view biblical authority as a correlative to Christ's lordship. James Mosteller states that Scripture's authority is derived from the dynamic experience of Christ's lordship in the individual's life. He argues that the authority of the Bible is a derived authority, coming from the Lord. "The written Word derives its vitality from the Living Word. One does not believe in Jesus because he believes in the Bible; he believes in the Bible because he believes in Jesus." Mosteller contends that this understanding allows for a religious authority that transcends the Bible. Religious authority is founded upon the unmediated lordship of Christ. This lordship is guided and shaped by the Scriptures, particularly the New Testament. Christ's lordship is manifested in the believer through a responsible, individual interpretation of the Bible guided by the Holy Spirit.[21]

SIGNIFICANCE

All the writings on Baptist distinctives relegate the Bible to a unique place in the distinctive genre. Both the Reformation and Enlightenment traditions attribute some meaningful purpose to the Bible. Both traditions contend that Baptists are the only group that confers this unique status upon the Bible. Whereas other Christian denominations perceive creeds, councils, or religious traditions as authoritative, Baptists have a unique perspective of the Scriptures that distinguishes them from other Christian groups. Baptists are adamant in their belief that they alone consistently understand and submit to the authority of the Bible. This is even true in a limited measure for those writings that affirm the primacy of Christian experience over biblical authority.

These writings also reveal that Baptists differ in their precise definitions of religious authority. As demonstrated, some Baptists believe that the exclusive religious authority for Baptists is biblical authority. This perspective is found in the earliest writings of this theological genre and continues to enjoy strong support in Baptist life today.

Those Baptist distinctives found within the Enlightenment tradition differ from those found within the Reformation tradition. They posit some expression of Christian experience as essential for religious authority. The consensus is that the authority of the Bible is only one aspect of religious authority. Christian experience is either equal to or above the authority of the Bible. The historical teachings of the Bible become authoritative for the individual as the person experiences God.

Coupling Christian experience with biblical authority is a later development in the distinctive genre. Beginning with Mullins, Christian experience finds support among some Baptists who view this development as universally true of the distinctive theological identity of all Baptists. Supporters of this position typically advocate a diminished role for Scripture in religious authority.

Expressions of Christian experience vary in this tradition. Some argue for Christian experience in general, ambiguous terms. Other writings specifically advocate the lordship of Christ as that which is experientially authoritative. All in all, these writings contend that religious authority for Baptists is expressed primarily through Christian experience within the interpretative framework of the Bible. The Bible becomes primarily an interpreter or a guide to one's Christian experience. The Bible is authoritative as it provides direction and interpretation of one's experience of God.

The evidence does not support the notion that Christian experience has always been a part of religious authority within writings on Baptist distinctives. The tendency to join Christian experience together with biblical authority is a twentieth-century occurrence. This particular understanding of Baptist distinctives is absent in the earlier writings and marks a shift in Baptist understanding of religious authority.

CHAPTER FIVE

A Distinctive Church

Having examined the epistemological component of Baptist distinctives, I will now examine the ecclesiological component; that is, the distinctive genre's perspectives on the doctrine of the church. The following three chapters will investigate three doctrinal tenets commonly found in this genre. Baptists argue that their unique ecclesiology is most plain in their beliefs of a regenerate church membership, baptism, and congregational polity.

These convictions are not in and of themselves peculiar to the Baptists. Baptists do claim, however, a distinctive expression of these doctrines in two ways. First, their doctrine of the church is distinctive because their ecclesiology is always shaped and directed by the New Testament. Baptists desire to construct a church as closely as possible to the "primitive" churches described in the New Testament. Second, Baptists recognize that these doctrinal tenets are found in other Christian denominations. It is argued, however, that the combination of these items as an expression of New Testament authority is found only in Baptist life.

Baptists believe that each congregation most resembles the New Testament model when it is comprised and governed by those who claim Jesus Christ as Lord and Savior and covenant together to practice their faith in voluntary assembly. Baptists contend that only those who have been regenerated by the Holy Spirit through a voluntary faith in Christ and who have professed their faith in personal confession and baptism are scripturally qualified for church membership.

I need to make a few qualifications. The Baptist understanding of a regenerate church membership is not a claim that every Baptist is converted or that every Baptist church has a pure, regenerate membership. Many unconverted people, some honestly misled about their faith and others more deceptively intentioned, are unfortunately counted among the members of Baptist churches. Further, this emphasis upon a regenerate church membership is not a judgment that all other non-Baptist Christians are unconverted. Baptists do not claim that they are the only Christians in the world. The general consensus in distinctive writings is simply that Baptist principles, when consistently applied, will theoretically exclude from church membership all but the converted.

Writings on Baptist distinctives assert that the formal, theological principles of other denominations allow for individuals who are not born again to become members of their churches. These churches, by having doctrines that allow the unregenerate into church membership, cannot be considered "pure, spiritual" churches; that is, true New Testament churches. Baptists assert that their distinctives are the only doctrines that logically and inevitably lead a church to be a pure, spiritual body of believers in Christ.

A REGENERATE CHURCH IN THE REFORMATION TRADITION

For some Baptists, the doctrine of a regenerate church is the only way to create true, New Testament churches. For example, John Quincy Adams argues that Baptists are truer to the model of the "primitive church" established in the New Testament than any other Christian denomination. In conjunction with New Testament teaching, Baptists believe that those who gladly "received the word" are also those "immersed on the profession of their faith." Baptists base their understanding of a regenerate church membership upon the biblical model of the New Testament church.

> Baptists regard the kingdom of Christ as a purely spiritual organization, separate and distinct from the world. Acting upon this conviction, they admit none to baptism and membership, but such as profess their faith in Jesus, and give satisfactory evidence that they have "passed from death unto life." They recognize no hereditary claims to the covenant of grace. . . . They aim to show that Christ's "kingdom is not of this world." They receive none but professed converts, and when these walk disorderly, they withdraw themselves from them. They are laboring to reform both Protestant and Papal Christendom on this point, which they regard of vital importance to the best interests of the church and the world. Let their principles prevail, and there can be no

unhallowed union of Church and State, no amalgamation of Christ's kingdom with the world; but the Church, with undiminished lustre will shine forth, her glory unobscured, her ordinances uncorrupted, and her membership uncontaminated, and instead of being "the mistress of the State," or the courtesan of the world—as pedobaptism has in too many instances made her—she will appear in all her loveliness as the Bride of Christ![1]

A regenerate church serves to protect the church against doctrines detrimental to church life, such as infant baptism (also called pedobaptism in older writings). John Broadus argued that a church ought to consist "only of persons making a credible profession of conversion" in Christ. Broadus rejects infant baptism and asserts that only those people capable of making their own profession of faith should be considered for church membership. This conviction applies equally to adults and to children. Infant baptism is "alien to the genius of Christianity, not only unsupported by the New Testament but in conflict with its essential principles." Only those persons who are capable and do give credible evidence of conversion should be received as church members. Those who do not lead a godly life or fail to show one's faith by good works should either be rejected in the appeal for membership or be excluded from membership through "strict church discipline."[2]

J. M. Pendleton takes the argument a step further. He notes that the doctrine of a regenerate church and the doctrine of infant baptism are mutually exclusive. Pendleton suggests that "Baptists are distinguished from all other religious denominations by their belief that no one is eligible to a church relation who has not first been brought into a

personal, spiritual relation to Christ by faith in his name."
Baptists hold to the scriptural order that a person must come
first to Christ and then to the church and its ordinances. Faith
is the most personal of acts and cannot be received by proxy
or unconsciously. For Pendleton, the practice of infant baptism is the antithesis of the doctrine of a regenerate church.
Either the practice of infant baptism is true, or the necessity
of a regenerate church membership is true; both views cannot
be true. They are irreconcilable.

> In this belief we see such a divergence of views between
> Baptists and others as makes compromise and harmony
> impossible. The question is broad and deep, embracing
> the New Testament doctrine of a spiritual church. If
> Pedobaptists are right in their conception of a church,
> Baptists are wrong; if Baptists are right, Pedobaptists are
> wrong. The antagonism between them is not incidental
> or accidental, but essential and inevitable. It may be
> said—it need not be said in any offensive sense—that
> the antagonism involves a war of extermination. That is
> to say, if the Pedobaptist view of a church and its ordi-
> nances should be so carried into effect as to attain uni-
> versal prevalence, the Baptist view would be banished
> from the earth; if the Baptist view of a church and its
> ordinances should universally prevail, the Pedobaptist
> view must become obsolete. The two views are destruc-
> tive of each other.[3]

The practice of infant baptism either presupposes that infants
are truly regenerated and they are church members, or that
infants who are baptized are unregenerated and yet still are
regarded as members. If the former is true, then faith either lacks
any elements of conscious, personal volition, or faith is irra-
tional. If the latter is true, then conversion is not a prerequisite

for entrance into the community of faith. Pendleton, along with most Baptists, finds both of these options objectionable. The essence of the spiritual dynamic of the Baptist view of the church is expressed in a personal understanding of faith. Any other understanding of faith denies the biblical model for a regenerate church and changes the order of the process of church membership.

> A New-Testament church is a spiritual brotherhood, the members of which are the subjects of spiritual life, and the ordinances of the gospel are designed for spiritual persons. The opposite view is fraught with evil, for it changes the order which Christ has established. It permits persons to come to the church and its ordinances before they come to Christ. Baptists regard this as disastrous heresy, and utter their earnest protest against it. They have stood alone in the centuries past, and they stand alone now, in advocacy of the great principles, CHRIST FIRST, THEN THE CHURCH AND ITS ORDINANCES.[4]

Another benefit Baptists see in this doctrine is that it protects the church from moral impurity. J. B. Jeter argues that the foundation of the Baptist understanding of the church is a regenerate church membership. Baptists follow the model of "the primitive churches," which "were composed of believers, and of believers only, and all the facts recorded in the inspired history and all the instructions in the inspired epistles are in perfect harmony with this fundamental principle of church organization." The natural tendency of infant baptism is to obliterate "the distinction between the world and the church." The result of failing to emphasize a regenerate church membership is that:

in most every land where pedobaptism has enjoyed uncontrolled sway, the limits of the church and the world have been coextensive. All the infidelity, corruption, and blasphemy of the people have been within the church. Its discipline has been overthrown, or exercised only in regard to those who have questioned its authority.[5]

The integrity of the church's message is protected by the doctrine of a regenerate church. Alvah Hovey is concerned to keep the church and the world separate. For him, infant baptism introduces elements of the unregenerate into the church, thereby making the church as corrupt and as evil as the world. The biblical mandate of a regenerate church safeguards the relevance and effectiveness of the church in its gospel proclamation to a fallen world. The church's witness is diminished or destroyed when the world's corruption is permitted within a church. When this doctrine is forsaken or modified, the world overcomes the church and diminishes the kingdom work of God.[6]

Certain Baptists use a regenerate church to underscore the spiritual vitality of its members and the spiritual work of God. B. H. Carroll argues that the church is a "spiritual body. None but the regenerate should belong to it." Whereas other Christian denominations believe that the church is the place where salvation is given, Carroll notes that the church "is not a savior, but the home of the saved." The church cannot regenerate a person through the ordinances. Regeneration occurs only by God's act through grace.

Carroll suggests that the doctrine of a regenerate church is useful in two ways. First, it destroys sacramentalism (the idea that grace is somehow conveyed through religious rituals) and sacerdotalism (the notion that ordination gives a person the ability to administer religious rituals). Second, it "draws a line of cleavage between the church and the world."[7] The spiritual quality that a church enjoys radically distinguishes its purpose and nature from other worldly entities.

A regenerate church demonstrates for some Baptists the authority of the New Testament for right belief. George McDaniel states that the witness of the New Testament is for a regenerate church membership. He notes that infant baptism is not taught within the Scriptures. He further argues that it undermines the need for conversion as a prerequisite for membership:

> There is absolutely no evidence that baptism was administered except upon a voluntary profession of faith. If it is permissible to take into the church one unconverted, then it is permissible to take into the church all unconverted and thereby to have churches composed entirely of unbelieving sinners. We demand repentance and faith before baptism.[8]

Failure to adhere to a regenerate church membership not only undermines the conversion of the membership but also, according to McDaniel, promotes heresy:

> The belief that baptism was essential to salvation and that infants dying unbaptized were lost facilitated the growth of infant baptism. . . . The heresy spread and became the prolific parent of an unregenerated church membership, of the servitude of the individual to an institution, of the union of Church and State and of persecution for conscience sake. It remains the bulwark of Romanism and the most insurmountable barrier to Christian union.[9]

In this way a regenerate church defends against deviant doctrinal beliefs about God and his saving work through Jesus Christ.

The ability to live and function as a true, vibrant member of a church requires this emphasis on a regenerate church. W. R. White maintains that a church based upon the teachings of the New Testament should be "composed of born-again, baptized believers." The ability to function within a spiritual community presupposes a spiritual regeneration. A New Testament church mandates regeneration in order for an individual to function within the community of faith. No unregenerate person can be a member or practice the spiritual disciplines necessary for church membership and life. This rationale excludes infants incapable of exercising their own faith and thereby receiving God's regenerating work. "Irresponsible infants are incapable of any conscious participation in or appropriation of the life and activities of a church. It is literally impossible for them to be members."[10]

The personal nature and necessity of the new birth is identified as an integral component of the doctrine of a regenerate church. Herbert Gezork argues that the church as expressed in Baptist thought is built upon the regeneration of its members. The nature of this regeneration is one of personal conversion, of personal commitment, of personal confession of faith. "The Christian life begins always where an individual soul experiences Christ as Savior and surrenders to Him as Lord." Surrender to Christ as Lord is that which places a person into the membership of the church. This understanding of regeneration and church membership leads Gezork to reject infant baptism.

> Such is our rejection of infant baptism. We reject it on the one hand because of our conception of the Church as a fellowship of believers in Christ. But we reject it also because we refuse to join a child to the Church before he can utter his protest or give his consent. Thus

we regard infant baptism as an intolerable invasion of the sphere of man's own most sacred religious rights.[11]

A regenerate church membership ensures the effective performance of a church in its ministry responsibilities. Henry Cook states that, according to Baptists, the church "is a society of believers united to Christ by personal faith, and directed in their work and witness by His indwelling Spirit." If biblical teaching is consistently followed, membership into a church is predicated upon the regeneration of the person. Regeneration is the means whereby the privileges and responsibilities of church life are attained. Although Baptists may differ on many other points, Cook contends that Baptists have offered a united front on this point. He maintains that true Christian unity will not prevail until all Christian denominations advocate the doctrine of a regenerate church membership. "Not until Christendom returns to the simple and straightforward conception of the Church as we have it in the teaching of the New Testament can we hope to get rid of all the confusion that undoubtedly exists in the mind of the average man."[12]

Jack Hoad perceives that a regenerate church is inherent within the Great Commission to make disciples. He insists that Baptists believe that the church is "the gathered company of regenerate persons in any locality, each of whom has evidenced his spiritual life by a personal repentance of sin towards God and faith in the Lord Jesus Christ for salvation." He argues that only those persons who have professed their regeneration should be the recipients of baptism. This argument excludes the baptism of infants and includes only those who, through regeneration, are "aware of sins" and have "turned from them, believing in Jesus Christ for salvation as proclaimed in the gospel." In no sense would this New Testament understanding include unregenerate persons, either adult or infant.

The Great Commission itself rules out the validity of infant baptism and so does the first documented fulfillment of that Commission recorded in Acts 2 which reflects the evidence of regeneracy in the felt need for forgiveness of sin and the response to the gospel in repentance and obedience in baptism. Hence baptists [sic] demand that the subjects of baptism must be regenerate.[13]

Hoad perceives that submission to the "baptist principle" of strict obedience to the New Testament and adherence to a regenerate church membership would result in the cessation of a distinctive Baptist identity because all denominations would, in a sense, be "baptistic."

A REGENERATE CHURCH IN THE ENLIGHTENMENT TRADITION

Walter Rauschenbusch states that the essence of the Christian faith is in "spiritual experience." Persons are summoned to repent consciously from sin and receive forgiveness. True church membership and true church ministry are based upon this religious experience. "If anyone desires to enter our churches we ask for evidence of such experience and we ask for nothing else. . . . Experience is our sole requisite for receiving baptism; it is fundamental in our church life." Other Christian denominations structure church membership on "adulterated" forms of religious "ritual and sacrament." Baptists, however, set forth the purest expression of church life by their insistence upon a "personal," "free," and "moral" regeneration.[14]

John Freeman states that the doctrine of a regenerate church emphasizes the close connection between the believer and Christ.

> Since the Church is Christ's body, membership in the
> Church should depend upon, follow and express a pre-
> vious personal relation to Him as the incorporating and
> directing Head. To admit to the body those who are not
> joined to the Head by a living faith, is to commit a mis-
> chievous incongruity.[15]

Baptists adhere to the doctrine of a regenerate church membership because it serves as a safeguard for the intrusion of
"unregenerate-life" within the church. Infant baptism threatens the vitality and effectiveness of the church in its gospel
proclamation to the world. The practice of infant baptism
should "be discontinued and entirely discarded as an out-
worn tradition, and shunned as a garment spotted by the
flesh."

E. Y. Mullins expresses his understanding of a regenerate
church membership in terms of the sovereign initiative of God.
The Holy Spirit creates the church through His "sovereign
agency." The Holy Spirit determines the "spiritual environment"; that is to say, entrance into the church is at God's initiative and not "human agency." This sovereign act of God is
expressed historically in the regeneration of persons. The
"renewed spiritual natures" of these persons then compels
"them to associate themselves together as a church."

Mullins's definition of a church begins with the initiating
act of the Holy Spirit, drawing persons together through regeneration. Their regeneration then compels their voluntary association together in fellowships called churches. The indwelling
Spirit organizes the membership of Christ's body into his
church. "Human actions" which promise entrance into the fellowship of a church offer empty hopes. Mullins cites infant
baptism as one such human action. Since infant baptism is of
human initiative and not of the Spirit's initiative, the practice

only serves to introduce unregenerated persons into the abode of the "indwelling Spirit."[16]

Philip Jones sees soul competency best expressed in a regenerate church emphasis. Since the soul is capable and responsible to relate directly to God, the composition of the membership of the church should reflect this conviction. Regeneration shapes not only the nature of the church but also the nature of the church's ministries and ordinances. The nature of Christian ministry, Christian discipleship, and Christian baptism are all corollaries to the doctrine of a regenerate church membership. Jones further argues that the strict adherence of Baptists to the absolute insistence upon a regenerate church membership should be viewed as the exclusive soteriological contribution of Baptists to the evangelical world.[17]

James Kirtley likewise sees an intimate connection between a regenerate church and soul competency. For him, the introduction of five "interferences" results in the loss of soul competency, thereby impeding the biblical teaching of regeneration. These theological intrusions into Christianity are: baptismal regeneration, infant baptism, a papal hierarchy, union of the church and the state, and removal of the Bible from the people. All these entities in some form or another impose an "interference" between the individual and God. The elimination of these would result in the reclamation of Baptist distinctives and therefore a reclamation of the personal dynamic of regeneration. Although Kirtley surveys briefly the historical impact of the five "interferences" upon Christianity, he does not address the implications of the doctrine of regeneration for church membership.[18]

George Horr sees the importance of this doctrine in terms of its ability to "vindicate" the truthfulness of the Scriptures and of the "Christian system." He advocates the position that the emphasis upon regeneration is peculiar primarily to

Baptists. He deviates somewhat from his predecessors in his explication of regeneration. He is not overly concerned with discussing the significance of regeneration for church membership. Rather, the experience of regeneration is the means by which the personal blessings of the Christian life are received. The conviction of the authoritative nature of Scripture is also obtained via regeneration. "This emphasis upon the regenerate life and upon Christian experience indicates the process by which all the great Christian doctrines are vindicated."[19]

H. Wheeler Robinson develops his notion of a regenerate church membership from his understanding of believer's baptism. "If baptism be the accepted and generally recognized mode of entrance into the visible Church, . . . then to confine it to believers is to assert in the plainest and most unmistakable way that personal faith is the most essential element in religion." Regeneration implies a changed nature, a new heart, a surrendered will. The outward ceremony of believer's baptism signifies the inner change brought through regeneration.

Robinson does not develop the significance of regeneration for church membership. He instead articulates the doctrine of regeneration primarily in individual terms. Regeneration is "the best safeguard" for the "individuality of faith" and is a "lonely," yet "unique experience." He does concede that regeneration carries implications for the community life of a church as well as society as a whole. Robinson nevertheless laments that the "modern social emphasis" in religion tends to obscure the "primary foundation of religion"; that is, the individual experience of personal regeneration.[20]

James Rushbrooke interprets the personal regeneration of the individual as a voluntary surrender to Christ's lordship. Individual regeneration is "for us the royal dominant fact." He asserts that only through the experience of personal regeneration can an individual be made a Christian. He therefore construes the Baptist ideal of the church as "the voluntary but inevitable association of faithful men, each in immediate relation with his lord, spiritual equals in Christ." Rushbrooke develops his understanding of the personal regeneration of the individual for church polity, but he gives only a truncated mention of the implications of regeneration for church membership.

> We believe in the Church universal, the only church that is catholic without qualification. It is a Divine, a supernatural, and a continuous creation. It embraces all the faithful. Its unity is indestructible; and into it as living stones are built all true Christians. That Church is not an institution; it transcends them all; none of them, nor all together, can fully represent it. But it is certainly by the will of Christ and inspiration of His Spirit that Christian men come together in visible societies. When we call their association "voluntary," we mean that it is the personal act of each believer; and that this spiritual fellowship cannot be entered by proxy, nor under external constraint.[21]

James Mosteller understands the doctrine of a regenerate church encapsulating all that the church is to be and do. He suggests that "the principle as to the nature of the church" is that it is "to be composed of those 'gathered' (by the Holy Spirit and regenerated), 'separated' (from the state and society) by the badge of baptism, 'disciplined' (by the use of the Supper and internal examination, not externally by the state), and 'commissioned' (to return to the world and witness)." The distinctive theological identity of Baptists rests upon this doctrine. It determines who may or may not rightfully belong to the church.

This doctrine is most visibly expressed through the practice of believer's baptism. This visible sign is the touchstone of the true nature of the church. A regenerate church membership is the reason Baptists oppose infant baptism. He argues that the church should include only those committed voluntarily to Christ. Regeneration implies a volitional commitment to follow Christ. Since infants are incapable of a volitional response, they are not true subjects for regeneration and are ineligible for Baptist church membership.[22]

Wayne Ward's emphasis regarding regeneration is upon the experiential and personal dynamic of the life of discipleship. He notes that Baptists are not called "Baptists" because of their practice of immersion but "because they required an experience of repentance and faith before they would accept one for baptism." He stipulates that baptism was never intended as a religious ritual but rather as a sign of regeneration and Christian discipleship. Regeneration brings an individual into a "right relationship with God." This new, regenerated relationship is expressed in the act of baptism rather than the act of baptism serving as the means of attaining regeneration. Although he rejects the practice of infant baptism, he does not address the issue of the importance of regeneration for church membership.[23]

Justice Anderson states that the Baptist interpretation of a New Testament church as composed only of regenerate members is the "cardinal principle of Baptist ecclesiology." The Baptists' rejection of infant baptism, the practice of believer's baptism, the insistence upon congregational polity, and the various limitations upon participation in the Lord's Supper are "logical conclusions" of the doctrine of a regenerate church membership. Anderson's "ecclesiastical principle" asserts that the church is a "regenerate" community through which "Christ communicates his gospel and his commands." To emphasize a regenerate church membership does not mean "legalistic barriers of an exclusive, self-righteous church," but rather "stringent requirements" intended to "safeguard the purity" of the spiritual nature of the church.[24]

SIGNIFICANCE

The doctrine of a regenerate church as presented in distinctive writings advocates that all church memberships should be converted. Several common themes emerge from this survey and suggest a consensus of opinion for the Reformation and Enlightenment traditions. All agree in some regard that a regenerate church membership protects the purity and integrity of the church. The doctrine of a regenerate church preserves the individual's personal accountability to God and mandates the necessity of personal conversion. They also assert the importance of regeneration occurring prior to participation in the ordinances of baptism and the Lord's Supper. The practice of infant baptism is viewed by all as that which either threatens or destroys the credibility and effectiveness of a church. The distinctive writings also argue that Baptists are the best and truest expression of this particular doctrine.

Having noted the similarities between the two traditions, some differences of interpretation and emphasis do exist. As I assess the materials, the significance of the ordinances are somewhat diminished. Further, I see some fluidity in the Enlightenment tradition between the corporate and the individual. Authors such as Rauschenbusch, Freeman, Jones, Rushbrooke, Mosteller, and Anderson are concerned to demonstrate the importance of regeneration for the corporate life and nature of the church. The church's spiritual strength for ministry and witness is tied to this doctrine. Others, such as Mullins, Horr, Robinson, Kirtley, and Ward, are more prone to emphasize the importance of regeneration for individual religious experience. They develop the implications of a regenerate church for individual Christian living. In other words, the latter group is less likely to develop the corporate implications of regeneration and more prone to emphasize the individual benefits.

CHAPTER SIX

A Distinctive Ordinance

Distinctive writings frequently discuss the Baptist understanding of the ordinances. An ordinance is a practice established by Jesus Christ that commemorates some aspect of the Lord's atoning sacrifice or redeeming work. An ordinance differs from a sacrament in that the latter is believed to bring the participant into some sphere of grace. Ordinances are not considered to impart any type of grace.

Baptists traditionally advocate two ordinances: baptism and the Lord's Supper. Distinctive writings often discuss the ordinances as one expression of the ecclesiological component. On occasion, both baptism and the Lord's Supper are examined within the distinctive genre. More often than not, however, only baptism receives attention. There are a couple of reasons for this.

First, in most Christian denominations, the beliefs about the nature of one ordinance or sacrament are often the same for the other ordinances or sacraments. Baptists, since they hold to a memorial view of baptism, also advocate a memorial view of the Lord's Supper. Baptism is often regarded as the representative ordinance. Second, baptism is considered the ordinance marking the believer's entrance into church membership. The issue of a regenerate church membership, as previously discussed, naturally lends itself to the issue of who are the proper recipients of the rite of baptism and therefore, entrance into the church.

Baptist distinctives are not concerned simply to construct the theological meaning of the ordinances. Their discussions are intended to highlight the unique Baptist perspective in distinction to the positions of other Christian denominations. As will be evident, Baptists not only state what they believe about baptism, but they also engage and critique polemically what they perceive as deficiencies in other Christian denominations. This is especially true on the matter of infant baptism.

BAPTISM IN THE REFORMATION TRADITION

Baptist churches follow biblical teaching when they allow only immersed persons into their memberships. John Quincy Adams argues that the "primitive" churches were composed only of baptized believers. The mode of baptism is immersion.

> By baptized, I mean immersed believers. 'They that gladly received his word were immersed.' This is the translation—in the common version we have only a

transfer. . . . It is evident, also, from the narration of circumstances connected with baptism in the New Testament, that immersion was the primitive mode.

Adams states that only immersed persons were admitted into the membership of the churches. "All who became members of the primitive churches were admitted by immersion; and as none were admitted but believers, none but believers were immersed."[1]

Baptism is also an act of submission and obedience to Christ. For John Broadus, baptism must be practiced according to "Christ's commands." The mode is not what makes baptism significant. Its significance is rather found in its compliance with Scripture's guidelines. Broadus outlines three important features regarding baptism. First, the element employed, water, represents purification. Second, the action performed, dipping, represents burial and resurrection, "picturing the burial and resurrection of Christ, and symbolizing the believer's death to sin through faith in Christ and his resurrection to walk in newness of life." Third, performing the ceremony should be in the name of the Lord Jesus and the Father and the Holy Spirit. Baptism is an "oath of allegiance, a vow of devotion to Jesus Christ, to the Triune God."[2]

For some Baptists, true baptism is a defining trait of a true church. J. M. Pendleton's doctrine of baptism has two primary emphases. The doctrine of baptism must rest upon scriptural teaching and faithfully portray the sacrifice of Jesus Christ. He cites Greek lexicons that give "immerse," "dip," or "plunge" as the ordinary and literal meaning of the Greek term *baptizo*. He further notes that distinguished pedobaptist scholars concede that *baptizo* means "to immerse." The meaning of baptism as death, burial, and resurrection can only be conveyed through immersion. Pendleton contends that the historical testimony for more than thirteen hundred years supported the notion of baptism by immersion, except in cases of sickness and urgent necessity. The following quotation summarizes his understanding of the meaning of baptism.

> To conclude the argument from the design of baptism: How stands the matter? If baptism commemorates the burial and the resurrection of Christ, it must be immersion. If it is an emblematic representation of death to sin and resurrection to newness of life, the representation is essentially incomplete without immersion. If it symbolizes the remission of sins, the washing away of sins, and moral purification, the purposes of the symbol requires immersion. The fullness of the remission, the thoroughness of the washing, and the completeness of the purification demand an act affecting the whole body. If there is something in baptism that anticipates and resembles the resurrection of the dead, still it must be immersion. Sprinkling and pouring are as unlike a resurrection as they are unlike a burial.[3]

Baptism is also a necessary requirement for church membership. In fact, Pendleton goes so far as to suggest that "an unimmersed congregation, . . . even if a congregation of believers, is not a New-Testament church. . . . There can be no visible church without baptism." For Pendleton, baptism is a sign of a true church and a manifestation of true repentance and faith.[4]

T. T. Eaton shares Pendleton's conviction that baptism by immersion serves as a sign for a true, New Testament church. Using the New Testament as the basis for his argument, Eaton argues that the mode of baptism must be immersion. "Baptists affirm that New Testament baptism is the immersion in water in the name of the Trinity of a believer on a profession of his faith by one duly set apart by a church for such a service." He further argues that only persons able to profess faith in Christ should be baptized. Consistent adherence to the Bible eliminates the practice of baptizing infants. "Baptists hold that the Bible teaches that believers in Christ and none others are to be baptized. No example or precept for baptizing infants can be found in the Word of God, and the advocates of infant baptism do not claim any such example or precept." Only those churches which practice baptism by immersion for entrance into church membership are true, New Testament churches.[5]

Baptism symbolizes God's purifying of the believer. *Baptist Why and Why Not* asserts that the act of baptism represents "purification, indeed, but total purification through the regenerating power of the Holy Spirit, purification always connected with its procuring cause in the name of the Lord Jesus Christ, and so the believer's union with Christ in His death, burial and resurrection." The element and the act utilized in the rite of baptism are both symbolic. "The element is water and stands for purification, the act is an immersion, followed in the nature of the cause, by an emersion [sic], the one standing for a burial (which implies of course a death) and the other for a resurrection."

The symbolic nature of the ordinance proclaims saving faith. It does not produce it. It expresses repentance, but it does not acquire it. Infant baptism is rejected because the Bible only authorizes the baptism of believers. Infants are incapable of exercising their own faith; thus, they should not be the recipients of the ordinance. Baptists oppose infant baptism because of "the vicious error that lay under it, viz.—the doctrine of baptismal regeneration." Infant baptism develops "the mischievous idea that any one dying without the waters of baptism went straight to the flames of torment." In response to the contention that Baptists make too much of baptism, those who adhere to infant baptism make more of baptism than Baptists. Baptists "make no more of it and no less of it than the Scriptures require."[6]

Baptism is both a condition for membership and a symbolic ordinance. J. B. Jeter notes that Baptists are not unique in requiring baptism for church membership. In fact, all Christian denominations require in some form baptism for membership.

> No evidence, or semblance of evidence, can be furnished from the Scriptures that any person was ever received into an apostolic church without baptism. Indeed, there is no point concerning which Christians of all denominations and parties are more united than in maintaining the necessity of baptism to church membership. There is no large and settled church or sect that does not make baptism a condition of admission to its privileges.[7]

With regard to the issue of a symbolic ordinance, baptism as immersion conveys several figurative meanings that sprinkling or pouring cannot convey, such as burial and washing. For Baptists, the ordinance is of utmost importance as an expression of one's conversion. Although the rite of baptism is not essential for salvation, obedience is.

> While we admit that baptism is not essential to salvation, we maintain that obedience is. Christ is "the author of eternal salvation unto all them that obey him"; and only unto such. Heb. v. 9. Baptism is a divine commandment, obligatory on all believers. It is enforced, not only by the supreme authority, but by the winning example of the Son of God. Of persons; ignorant, or misinstructed, or in doubt, or dilatory in regard to the ordinance, we say nothing. We leave them in the hands of a righteous Judge. Suppose, however, a person

professing to trust in Christ believes immersion to be divinely commanded, and deliberately and persistently refuses to submit to it; can he be saved? We judge not. He will be lost, not for the lack of baptism, but because his disobedience will demonstrate his want of faith, and consequently his unregeneracy. His rejection of baptism proves his disloyalty to the King of kings.[8]

To follow Christ is to follow his ways. His ways include submission to baptism by immersion both as a profession of faith and as entrance into the community of faith.

B. H. Carroll states that baptism is an ordinance that is "figurative and commemorative." Four elements are inherent within baptism, and these elements validate for him the importance and meaning of baptism. First, baptism can only be observed by proper authority, which is compliance with the New Testament. Further, the subject of baptism must be a repentant believer, a saved person. Also, the act of baptism must be immersion. Finally, the intent of baptism is to declare or confess one's faith, "symbolizing the cleansing from sin and commemorative of the resurrection."[9]

Baptism serves as the rite of entrance into the membership of a church. For George McDaniel, it is the "initial Christian ordinance." He equates baptism with immersion and obedience. The one measure of true Christian obedience to Christ's command is found in the mode of baptism. It is one of the first major acts of obedience that a Christian makes. Since Christ commanded baptism by immersion, to disregard the mode is disobedience to Christ's command.

McDaniel further notes that this obedience is an act of submission to the authority of the Bible. The rite of baptism is by immersion. The New Testament mode is by immersion. No biblical evidence exists for baptism by sprinkling or pouring.

To disregard immersion was for McDaniel to disobey the Bible's teachings. He further advocates three fundamental truths embodied in baptism. Baptism proclaims the fact of Christ's death and resurrection. It also declares the inward regeneration of the individual in the identification of the person with Christ's death and resurrection. Finally, baptism points to the future bodily resurrection from the dead.[10]

Baptism has no valid, biblical meaning apart from a saving experience with Christ. For W. R. White, baptism without a conscious, willful decision to follow Christ makes no sense. He asserts that baptism does not save. It is, however, closely connected with salvation. Baptism is associated with faith, repentance, prayer, and cleansing from sin. It is a symbolic picture of salvation. White contends that the mode of baptism is immersion. He rejects both infant baptism and baptismal regeneration.

> Belief in baptismal regeneration is the background that provided infant baptism. Most of the denominations now practicing infant baptism repudiate such an idea, but their older creedal statements reflect a belief in baptismal regeneration. All of these ideas are of Catholic origin. Infant baptism is given a totally different meaning today to that of the original significance, but it still is contrary to our definition of believer's baptism.[11]

Henry Cook argues that the significance of baptism is found in its connection to church membership. "Baptism occupied an important place in the witness and practice of the New Testament Church. It was regarded as the inevitable concomitant of Church membership, and it is unlikely that anyone was admitted to the Church's fellowship without it." The subjects of baptism are believers who were capable of professing their own faith. Infants are therefore excluded in the New Testament from this rite. Baptism is symbolic in its outward declaration of an inward conversion.

> The only question involved is the candidate's personal profession of faith in Christ, of which Baptism is intended to be the outward and visible sign. Baptism as Baptists see it is meant for believers and believers only, and they are convinced that the New Testament speaks with one voice on that point.[12]

The mode of baptism for Cook is immersion. "Immersion was the form of Baptism in its pre-Christian days, and it remained in Baptism all through the New Testament times."

Robert Baker defines the ordinance of baptism as a "meaningful symbol of Christian experience and reminders of the Christ who died that men might live." Baptism is not "magical"; the water does not wash sins away nor does it dispense grace. Baptism is rather the immersion in water of a saved person to symbolize his death to sin and resurrection to a new life in Christ. As one of two ordinances entrusted to the church, baptism serves as the rite that initiates a believer into the membership of a fellowship of a local church.[13]

Some Baptists perceive baptism as the first step of discipleship. Jack Hoad contends that Baptists practice baptism because the rite is commanded in Scripture "as the first act of a believer's discipleship and it is a once for all act of obedience . . . never to be repeated." The proper subject of baptism is a person "who is aware of sins and has turned from them, believing in Jesus Christ for salvation as proclaimed in the gospel." The mode of baptism is immersion of the believer in water.

> For the baptist [sic], baptism signifies the previous entrance of a believer into communion with his Lord and Saviour Jesus Christ, both in his death and his

resurrection, by which means newness of life has come to a formerly spiritually dead sinner. It declares that regeneration has taken place through union with Christ and he is now alive to God. It is therefore a symbol.[14]

BAPTISM IN THE ENLIGHTENMENT TRADITION

Walter Rauschenbusch is rather ambiguous on his meaning of baptism. He defines *baptism* as a "ritual of experience." Following the traditional Baptist position, he rejects baptismal regeneration and infant baptism. These understandings of baptism place human intrusions between the individual and God. They have human beings performing deeds that merit grace from God. Thus, humans begin to depend on other human beings for their salvation. This interference jeopardizes a personal, unmediated spiritual experience of God. For Rauschenbusch, baptism finds its significance as the "outgrowth" of personal experience. In other words, baptism is the "creed" or the "ritual" of the spiritual experience of the individual. It is a testimony of the believer's spiritual experience.

Rauschenbusch, however, never explains exactly what the believer has experienced. Further, he provides no rationale for why baptism should be by immersion, or, for that matter, the basis for the practice of baptism. He simply concedes the practice and connects the rite to "spiritual experience."[15]

John Freeman discusses the significance of the practice of baptism in his broader discussion of a regenerate church membership. Baptism is a sign only for those who have been born again. "Baptism is the symbol of regeneration, and must be reserved for those who, in personal confession of His name, put on the Lord Jesus Christ." The mode of baptism is by immersion because "the Master chose that form as the symbol of that death and resurrection by which He achieved His sovereignty, as well as of that death to sin and resurrection to newness of life by which the believer comes under His sovereign sway." For Freeman, the practice of infant baptism has no biblical basis and should be rejected as a grave danger to the spiritual, regenerate nature of Christ's church.[16]

E. Y. Mullins weaves his understanding of the doctrine of baptism throughout his work on Baptist distinctives. He notes that baptism is primarily symbolic, or "vocal," in its meaning. It has no sacramental or "magical" significance. Baptism neither contains nor imparts saving grace. For Mullins, detailed exegesis of the Scriptures results in the position that baptism should be administered only to believers as a profession of faith. Infants are not capable of such professions and therefore are not candidates for baptism.

> This ceremony [baptism] applied to infants also proceeds upon the assumption that the Church is like the State and that natural birth entitles to membership in it. It is too well known to require elaborate proof here that in this, as in other respects, Christ's Church is radically different from the State.[17]

Baptism derives its validity from the New Testament. Mullins therefore rejects the practice of infant baptism because it is based upon a nonvalid authority, namely, human tradition. Scripture mandates the practice of baptizing only believers. Mullins also stipulates that the writers of the New Testament assume that baptism precedes church membership. Baptists are therefore obligated to follow this assumption. Whereas sprinkling as a means of baptizing "destroys the meaning of the ordinance," Mullins explains that Baptists practice baptism by immersion because the mode "is urged as the Scriptural form of baptism and insisted upon as a duty."[18]

Baptism is primarily a symbolic ritual. Philip Jones argues that the symbolism of baptism is determinative for its meaning. "Only in immersion is the symbolism of the removal of sin preserved." Baptists have always had this understanding of baptism because the symbolism preserves the identification of the believer with Christ's burial and resurrection. "The symbolism of the baptism . . . is the burial of the old and a resurrection of the new, as well as the setting forth of Christ and his arising."[19]

H. Wheeler Robinson provides a detailed explanation of the doctrine of baptism. He argues that the original mode of baptism was immersion. "But no one has the right to argue that the baptism of the New Testament is less than the immersion of intelligent persons, as the expressive accompaniment of their entrance into a new life of moral and spiritual relationship to God." Baptism was symbolic in its meaning.

> The baptism of believers by immersion has not only emphasized conscious faith as essential to the Church, but it has also, by its symbolism, constantly recalled men to the foundation of the Gospel in history, the death and the resurrection of Jesus Christ, which, as Paul argued, are represented in the act of the believer's immersion and his rising from the waters of baptism.[20]

Robinson downplays the mode of baptism by immersion. "The ancient mode may be defended on various grounds, especially that of its expressive character and its impressive influence; but if this were all, or even the chief point, there would be absolutely no justification for the existence of Baptists." Baptism's significance is rather found in several New Testament themes. Baptism implies a cleansing from sin. The practice also serves as a reminder to believers of the gift of the Holy Spirit. Further, only believers should receive it. Finally, baptism is a testimony to the experiential union of the believer with Christ. Robinson rejects infant baptism because of the inability of infants to volitionally believe in Jesus Christ. He prefers instead to speak of the baptism of believers and not the baptism of adults.

> Nothing shows more clearly a failure to understand the faith of the Baptists than the frequent idea that they are a peculiar sect that insists on baptizing "adults" by immersion. They baptize not "adults" but "believers" on profession of their personal faith in Christ, and this is their primary distinction, though it has a very important bearing on the constitution of the Church into which such believers enter by their faith.[21]

In the New Testament, the acceptance of baptism implied the personal, individual conversion of the believer. Robinson rejects any notions that support any idea of baptismal regeneration. He also views baptism as the "door of entrance" into the church.

James Kirtley argues for a symbolic meaning in his understanding of baptism. It is a symbol given by Jesus of the death and resurrection to serve as a profession of the believer's faith in Jesus Christ. Baptismal regeneration destroys the true, biblical meaning of the ordinance.

> In being baptized one is preaching the gospel in a living tableau, saying, "This is a picture of what saves me, namely, the death of Christ for my sins and his resurrection for my justification." One is also telling one's Christian experience, saying, "This is a picture of the way it saved me, by my dying to sin and rising to a new life." One is also proclaiming one's hope of resurrection, saying in symbol, "This is a picture of what my body

shall experience when it is raised from the grave." But Christ's purpose was defeated when they made baptism a saving rather than a symbolical ordinance. Baptism is gone, even though the form might remain.[22]

Kirtley affirms that the mode of baptism was immersion in water. He categorically rejects any form of infant baptism or any view of baptismal regeneration. Baptism of only believers is the entrance into the life of the fellowship of believers.

Baptism is the outward symbol of the doctrine of a regenerate church membership. For James Rushbrooke, "The symbolism of immersion guards and proclaims great Evangelical truths and experiences: the saving significance of the death, burial, and resurrection of the Lord Jesus, the new life which is the common life of members of the Body of Christ." Baptism is the outward evidence of the inward submission to Christ's authority. Baptism of believers by immersion ensures "the simplicity and purity" of gospel proclamation and the necessity for personal acceptance of the gospel. Rushbrooke rejects the practice of infant baptism and refutes any notions of baptismal regeneration. Both are to be forsaken for their lack of scriptural foundation.[23]

James Mosteller addresses the significance of baptism in his broader discussion of the loss of the doctrine of a regenerate church membership among British Baptists. He laments the trend to practice "open membership." Open membership is the practice of allowing "non-immersed" Christians membership into Baptist churches without undergoing baptism by immersion. Mosteller argues that the church should be composed only of believers who have professed their faith publicly by immersion. The abandonment of this rite by British Baptists results in church memberships consisting of some persons who have been baptized as infants and yet have never professed their own faith in Christ. The result is the loss of a regenerate church membership and the loss of a distinctive trait of the theological identity of Baptists.[24]

Wayne Ward argues that baptism as described in the New Testament is symbolic, "the sign of identification as a follower of Jesus Christ." It is "the sign of an absolute break with an old life, and a resurrection to a new life." Only professing believers should be baptized. Baptizing infants cannot make them disciples of Jesus Christ. "Baptism can have a valid meaning only when it is the act by which a believer in Christ declares to the world his death to an old, sinful nature and his resurrection to walk in a new life with Christ."

Ward warns that baptism should not receive more emphasis than the ordinance was given by the New Testament. After citing 1 Corinthians 1:14 and 17, he states that these verses "should be a warning to us that baptism should not be exaggerated out of all importance and made to be the absolute necessity of the Christian life." Ward infers that the mode of baptism is immersion.[25]

Paul Beasley-Murray follows Robinson's understanding of the doctrine of baptism. He establishes the biblical basis for the rite in Christ's command, Christ's example, and the practice of the early church. He advocates a symbolic understanding for baptism. Baptism signifies: a union of the believer with Christ; a cleansing from sin; a confession of one's faith; a rite of initiation; and the Spirit's presence. Baptism is only for believers who are capable of professing their own faith in Christ. He also rejects infant baptism and baptismal regeneration. Like most British Baptists, Beasley-Murray downplays the significance of the mode of baptism.

> Although the symbolism of baptism naturally demands immersion, the distinctive aspect of the Baptist

approach to baptism is not the quantity of water but rather the quality of faith. If a choice has to be made, then the emphasis must be upon believer's baptism rather than on baptism by immersion.[26]

SIGNIFICANCE

Most of the distinctive writings within the Reformation tradition agree in meaning. They all affirm the necessity to conform the practice of baptism to the New Testament model and teaching. Only believers capable of professing their own faith personally should receive the ordinance. Baptism is the initiation rite of entrance into church membership and into the privileges of Christian ministry. All agree that the mode of baptism is immersion and is symbolic of the Christian experience of conversion. A strong emphasis is placed upon the significance of the rite of baptism for understanding the nature of the corporate life of the church. This includes the idea that baptism introduces the individual believer into the corporate life of the church body and that all those within the body jointly share the experience and blessings of spiritual regeneration.

All these writings reject infant baptism as a legitimate expression of New Testament baptism. Infant baptism undermines the necessity for a personal conversion experience and jeopardizes the uniqueness and the importance of a regenerate church membership.

The Enlightenment tradition shares many of the emphases found in the Reformation tradition. Areas of agreement include the symbolism of baptism, the distinctiveness of the ritual for Baptist identity, the rejection of infant baptism, and the administration of baptism to believers only.

Some different theological emphases do exist between the two traditions. The corporate implications of baptism as a rite of initiation into the membership of a church is not as consistently noted or developed by all the writings within the Enlightenment tradition. This is true of Rauschenbusch, Freeman, Mullins, Kirtley, Ward, and Beasley-Murray, just to name a few examples. Further, this tradition tends to focus more intently upon the personal implications of baptism and ignores or overlooks its significance for the corporate body. Some writings within the Enlightenment tradition downplay the importance of immersion as a necessary part of the symbolic meaning. In contrast, all Baptist distinctives within the Reformation tradition underscore the importance of the symbolic nature and meaning of immersion.

CHAPTER SEVEN

A Distinctive Polity

As I have already demonstrated, the doctrine of the church is of major importance in Baptist distinctives. The ecclesiological component has various expressions in this genre. In some instances, the focus of attention is on a regenerate church membership. On other occasions, the discussion revolves around the ordinances, particularly baptism. A third manifestation of the ecclesiological component is church polity.

Church polity is the organization, or governing structure, implemented within a local church. There are three major types of polity found in various Christian denominations today.

One form of polity is the Episcopal church government. This mode of church government locates the primary authority for decision-making in the office of the bishop. Power for decision-making may reside in the office of a single bishop, such as the pope in Roman Catholicism. Or, the decision-making prerogative may rest in a group of bishops. Another major type of church polity is Presbyterianism. The decision-making power in this structure resides in a group of elders. In the local church, this group forms the session. Select elders, or presbyters, from various churches in a certain geographical area form a presbytery. A third type of church polity is Congregationalism. This form of church government emphasizes the autonomy, independence, and authority of a local church. Individual members share equally together in decision-making.

Writings on Baptist distinctives all contend for Congregationalism as the most appropriate form of church government. These documents state that Baptist churches are closer to the New Testament model than any other Christian denomination with regard to church polity. In Baptist churches all members share equally in the affairs of the church. No member is considered any more or less important than any other member. All have responsibilities and privileges that are of equal significance in the life of the church.

Further, Baptists believe that each church is independent of every other church. Cooperation among the churches is encouraged and sometimes necessary. This cooperation, however, in no way implies one church exerting authority over the affairs of another church. No church, group of churches, convention, or association has any authority over any other church. Cooperation in Christian work is a voluntary privilege, not a requirement, of the churches of Jesus Christ. Baptist distinctives conclude that the only form of church government taught in the New Testament is Congregationalism.

Baptist distinctives attempt to highlight the Baptist understanding of congregational church government in distinction to the positions of other Christian denominations. This is typically done by comparing and contrasting Baptist polity with other denominational polities. In this manner, Baptist distinctives not only argue for the distinctive Baptist position on this issue, but they also reveal the polemical component at work in Baptist theology.

CHURCH POLITY AND THE REFORMATION TRADITION

The pattern of government found in a modern Baptist church should be reflective of the church government taught and modeled within the New Testament. According to John Quincy Adams, although other Christian denominations state that they adhere to a church polity based only on the New Testament, they in fact do not. Only the Baptists are faithful to obey the teachings of the New Testament with regard to church polity.

> All professed Christians, who admit that the Scriptures contain a model for church organization, strenuously maintain that the denomination with which they are connected, is formed after the Scriptural pattern. This is true alike of Episcopalians, Presbyterians, Methodists, and all others. But it is abundantly evident, that while these denominations are so very dissimilar, they cannot all resemble one Scriptural model. . . . The Fathers, Tradition, Expediency, are all pressed into their service, to supply the lack of evidence afforded in Scripture; or, as is sometimes the case, to nullify and render powerless its direct testimony against them. All this I say, is done by those who profess to find, in the New Testament alone, a warrant for their ecclesiastical systems and

organizations. They do not seem to perceive, that the
very course which they adopt to support their claims,
affords most conclusive evidence that they are false and
vain. But while some appeal to Tradition, and others to
expediency, it is the glory of the Baptists that they act on
the principle of the sufficiency of the Bible in testing this,
as well as all other questions relating to religion.[1]

Adams further advocates that the biblical model of church
polity as expressed in Baptist churches is the equality of all
members. He argues that the principles of church government
in the Baptist denomination are expressed in the text: "One is
your master, even Christ, and all ye are brethren." There is no
opportunity for the assumption of authority by a few. All members of the church "meet on the broad, even platform of equality." The rich and the poor, the minister, deacons, the laity are
all equal in status before God. A Baptist church is a place of
"perfect equality" in which all the members voluntarily enter
by their own choice. All members have privileges and benefits
that they share equally. The implementation of hierarchical
structures was to give to men an authority that belongs only to
Christ. The principle of equality applies not only to the laity
but also to the clergy, allotting to them the freedom to go to
new ministry opportunities if impressed to do so.

> The pastor, while he has no superior authority, has equal
> rights with the rest of his brethren. If called to go to
> another field of labor, he is at liberty to go without asking leave of a bishop, presbytery, or council. He is perfectly free to act in accordance with his own views of
> duty and his own convictions of right.[2]

Each church is autonomous in its relationships to other churches,
transacting its own business, exercising its own discipline, and

receiving and excluding its own members. Adams states that congregational polity gives every member of the church an equal right to speak and to vote.[3]

The New Testament teaches that the local churches are independent from one another. John Broadus states that no church has the biblical prerogative or authority to exert power or influence over another church. Churches are to seek out and engage in every opportunity for cooperation in benevolent, merciful ministry. Churches can also consult one another on questions of "truth and duty." These cooperative relationships, however, in no way allow one church to assume any authority over any other church. Broadus does not explicitly address the issue of congregational polity. He does give limited treatment to the necessity and the right of Baptist churches to exercise discipline upon those members who do not lead a godly life.[4]

Some Baptists believe that churches built upon the New Testament model will naturally be Baptist churches. J. M. Pendleton notes that each local church is autonomous from other local churches. No church is at liberty to interfere with the internal affairs of another. Any interdependence between churches is only in the sense of mutual fellowship. The ability to exercise church discipline and the appointment of officers by local churches as described in the New Testament further strengthens Pendleton's understanding of the autonomy of the local church. "Every Baptist church is an independent and a pure democracy. The idea of independence should be earnestly cherished, while that of consolidation should be as earnestly deprecated." He also contends that the biblical form of church government is congregational polity.

The independence of a church implies the right of a majority of its members to rule in accordance with the laws of Christ. . . . If, as has been shown, the governmental power of a church is with the members, it follows that a majority must rule—that is to say, either the majority or the minority must govern. But it is absurd to refer to the rule of the minority. That a majority must rule is so plain a principle of Independency, and so plain a principle of common sense, that it is needless to dwell upon it.[5]

Baptist Why and Why Not suggests that the institution of God's working in the world is a local church. Each church is independent of and autonomous from every other church. All ecclesiastical power is vested in each separate church. "The churches are wholly dependent on their Head and subject to His law, but independent of each other and of all other bodies whatsoever." Every church is directly related and subjected only to the head of the church, Jesus Christ. The polity of the Baptist church as taught by the New Testament is Congregationalism. New Testament churches are local, independent, and self-governing bodies. Every member is equal with every other. Each person is filled by the Spirit, united to Christ, and responsible to the Master. The Holy Spirit creates and operates the church by renewing each individual member, and the mind of the Spirit is made known through each individual composing the organization. Members are responsible to seek, to discern, and to report what they believed the Holy Spirit was making known to the local church.[6]

The polity of a Baptist church, as an expression of New Testament polity, should reflect the New Testament emphasis of a regenerate church membership. J. B. Moody disparages the polity of Episcopalian and Presbyterian churches. These models do not conform to New Testament teaching. Baptists practice congregational polity because the churches in the New Testament practiced congregational polity. The regenerated status of all the members of a local church requires a shared, equal authority between the clergy and the laity.[7]

Baptist churches practice what some call a "pure democracy." All the members of the church are equal citizens in Christ's kingdom, and the majority of the citizenry discerns the direction of God for the church. B. H. Carroll asserts that this polity is "of the people, for the people, and by the people." As a democracy, the church is responsible to receive members and to discipline members. Each church is further responsible to manage its own affairs. The ministers and members of the church are equal in status before God and in discernment of his will.[8]

Baptist churches are the truest expression of the New Testament teaching among all Christian denominations. For George McDaniel, the New Testament presents churches that are independent and self-governing. The decisions of each local church are final because there is no authority higher than that of a local church. Local churches can join together for certain ministries, but this bond is a union of a common faith and ministry. No church assumes any authority over the other in these joint, cooperative efforts.

Because each church is self-governing, each church also has control over its own membership. Churches can withdraw fellowship from members for just cause and restore members to fellowship upon repentance. No single minister should exert authority over the entire congregation. Each church is to elect its own ministers. McDaniel not only bases his understanding of Baptist church polity upon the New Testament but also upon a "sense of freedom and justice. As a minister . . . I should not like for the place and time of my pastorate to be determined by another man. As a layman, I should want some voice and vote in determining who was to be my pastor and how long he was to remain."[9]

Every believer has an equal right and an equal access to God through Christ. Distinctions between clergy and laity are "foreign" and "repugnant" to the Baptist understanding of the church. Each believer is responsible for seeking direction and wisdom from the Holy Spirit and expressing his convictions within the democracy of the local church. Since a spirit of independence characterizes each church member, each local church is independent from all other ecclesiastical structures or authorities.[10]

Baptist churches, more than any other Christian denomination, reflect accurately the New Testament's teaching concerning church polity. "New Testament churches are spiritual democracies. . . . All matters are referred to the congregations of the churches for settlements." The concept of the church as a democracy, however, does have limitations.

> The churches function for the kingdom of God in achieving the will of God on earth. However, they are democracies. Democracies functioning for a King and democracies under a Lord is what we have in our Baptist concept. Our churches are only democratic in certain relations. That is, each member is equal to every other member in sovereign rights and authority. The same is true of every church as related to other New Testament churches. In relation to Christ the church is not a democracy. It must be subject to his will as revealed in the New Testament and as experienced under the guidance of the Holy Spirit. The Lord has left, however, a large range of initiative to the churches as they are led by the Holy Spirit and as they keep within the boundaries of the New Testament principles. This is particularly true as to methods.[11]

To reject the concept of the church as a "pure democracy" would be for White a departure from the New Testament pattern and a violation of the democratic nature of the church. The priesthood of all believers eliminates any notion of a "priestly caste" and makes "democracy inevitable for the Lord's disciples." Each church is independent from all other ecclesiastical authorities.

Congregational polity as an expression of a regenerate church membership is a Baptist distinctive. The "independence" of a local church grants to each member an equal status and responsibility in the affairs of the church. Any distinctions between clergy and laity must be rejected. These distinctions violate the equality and brotherhood inherent within a New Testament church.

> No distinction between clergy and laity, as if the former were a special class, is recognized among Baptists. All members, men and women, whether ministers or not, are equal in their ecclesiastical standing. They constitute a brotherhood in which spiritual privileges are equally shared.[12]

Baptist understandings of independence do not mean rejecting any cooperative working among sister churches. Rather, Baptists work together for home and foreign missions, schools, benevolent institutions, and other common causes.

William Rone states that Baptists believe that the government of a New Testament church is democratic or congregational. The government of a local church is exercised by the whole membership as constituted of individual members. "The membership or constituency of each Church is entrusted with the duty and responsibility of carrying out the law and will of Christ expressed in the New Testament, under the leadership of the Holy Spirit, who inhabits and directs the affairs of Christ's Church." New Testament churches are independent of one another. "The Churches of the New Testament were separate and distinct from one another and each directed its own affairs independent of all others." Congregational polity and rejection of clergy/laity distinctions reflect the direct, unmediated headship of Christ over each local church.[13]

A Baptist church is a "self-governing community." The local church is enabled and responsible for the appropriate and godly government of itself by its membership. Each member shares in the direction and decisions of the affairs of the church. No external body, however influential or numerous, can impose on a Baptist church a decision that it does not choose to accept. Each church is the final arbiter in all matters that affect its well-being and destiny. Baptist churches are local, gathered communities that relate responsibly yet autonomously to other local, gathered communities for greater works of ministry.[14]

Baptists reject all authoritarianism other than that exercised directly by Jesus Christ through the Holy Spirit and the Scriptures. Instead, Baptists embrace "scriptural simplicity." The regenerate members of a local fellowship are to submit themselves to one another as members in equal standing. "The baptist [sic] recognizes the plurality of the gifts bestowed upon their churches, believing that each and every member has a God-given capability to contribute to the total ministry of the fellowship." No one church can exercise authority over another church. All are equal and independent of interference or control by other churches or groups of churches.[15]

CHURCH POLITY AND THE ENLIGHTENMENT TRADITION

Walter Rauschenbusch argues that Baptist churches are the most accurate reflections of New Testament polity in their self-governance, in their removal of clergy/laity distinctions, and in their mutual interdependence. He states that Baptist churches are self-governing democracies.

> Our churches are Christian democracies. The people are sovereign in them. All power wielded by its ministers and officers is conferred by the church. It makes ample room for those who have God-given powers for leadership, but it holds them down to the service of the people by making them responsible to the church for their actions. That democracy of the Baptist churches is something to be proud of.[16]

With regard to clergy/laity relations, Baptist churches recognize no priestly class. There is no essential difference between ministers and laity.

> We have no hierarchy within our ministry. We have no rector above the vicar, no bishop above the rector, no archbishop above the bishop, no pope above them all. Jesus bids us call no man father or master, but all of us are to be brethren, and the only greatness is to be by pre-eminent service. . . . That settles all hierarchies for me.[17]

The Roman Catholic authoritative elevation of the priest over the laity is "an inheritance from heathenism." With regard to the relation of one Baptist church to another, Rauschenbusch continues to affirm the "home rule" of each church. "Each church is sovereign in its own affairs." The self-government of churches, however, does not hinder them "from joining together with others in fraternal co-operation, in associations and state conventions, in city mission societies and national missionary organizations."

John Freeman argues for the abolition of ecclesiastical hierarchies because such structures suppress Christ's lordship in the spiritual experience of the individual believer. "The undelegated sovereignty of Christ renders it forever impossible that His saving grace should be manipulated by any system of man mediation." Any ecclesiastical governing structure that inhibits the mediatorial lordship of Christ jeopardizes the crown rights of the Son of God to interact personally in the life of the individual. "Any interposition of ecclesiastical machinery . . . is a manifest impertinence . . . and always a usurpation and a wrong."[18]

Some Baptists argue that polity should be derived from the Baptist conception of soul competency. E. Y. Mullins states that the competency of the regenerated individual implies a spiritual competency derived from the indwelling Christ. The authority of Christ is exerted in and through the inner life of believers. All human structures are rejected. "There is no conceivable justification, therefore, for lodging ecclesiastical authority in the hand of an infallible pope or bench of bishops." Democracy in church government is therefore an inevitable conclusion to the doctrine of soul competency.

> The independence and autonomy of the local church, therefore, is not merely an inference from a verse of Scripture here and there. It inheres in the whole philosophy of Christianity. Democracy in church government is simply Christ himself animating his own body through his Spirit. The decisions of the local congregation on ecclesiastical matters are the "consensus of the competent."[19]

The New Testament emphasis of an individual's relationship to God is Philip Jones's understanding of the polity of Baptist churches. He rejects all notions of clergy and laity distinctions. A church built upon the New Testament model is a democracy in which all members share equally in deciding the affairs of the church.

These elements of church organization are found in the New Testament, and beyond them there is no warrant for the intricate and elaborate ecclesiastical machinery that has been devised, nor for the absolute human authority it has sought to impose. The church to be true to its fundamental principles must be a democracy. The individual's relationship to God, the necessity of faith as a guide into the kingdom, and the priesthood and kingship of each believer, all demand the form of a democracy in which it shall stand before the world.[20] Such concepts are and must continue to be true of Baptist churches. Baptists have historically refused all attempts to impose ecclesiastical, authoritative structures over them, and Jones contends that they will continue to do so.

H. Wheeler Robinson sees an evolution of polity from the time of the Bible to the modern period. He notes that in the Bible there is very little evidence of democracy, or Congregationalism, and much evidence of the apostles exerting great influence by making decisions for the churches. Baptist churches now emphasize "the life of the Spirit," creating new forms of church polity to replace the biblical forms of polity. "Baptists hold, then, that the congregational polity of a Baptist Church is one legitimate way amongst others of expressing the fundamental idea of the Church." The self-governing independence of Baptist churches does not prevent their voluntary association. "From the beginnings of Baptist Church life in the seventeenth century right on to the present day successive forms of organization have been evolved to meet new needs, though the independence of the local Church was always jealously guarded and explicitly recognized."

The church is therefore not a "hierarchy of officials with an appendage of laymen" but rather a society of men and women sharing together in a corporate experience of Christian faith based on a common spiritual, individual experience. Robinson rejects any and all forms of distinction between clergy and laity. The intention of congregational polity is a means of protecting and ensuring the religious experiences of the individual members.[21]

The development of ecclesiastical hierarchy is an interference imposed upon the New Testament teaching of church polity. The localizing of power in a special priesthood promotes superstition within the church and limits the decision-making process. Based upon his understanding of religious experience and soul competency, James Kirtley rejects this development and argues that "if one person has as much inherent right as another to deal personally with God, then one group has as much right as another group, without overhead control from any man or set of men." He instead contends for a congregational understanding of church polity in which the authority resides entirely in the people composing the local group, not coming down from an overhead body but arising from the constituting body, a real democracy of soul.[22]

Baptist polity is unique in that it adheres to biblical teaching. Each individual church is a spiritual democracy under Christ. These individual churches may freely join with other churches in the work of the gospel. These joint ventures neither jeopardize nor diminish the autonomy or equality of the churches. They unite for mutual edification and for the discharge of the worldwide missionary tasks of the kingdom. Within each local assembly, individual believers are "competent under Christ" to share in the decisions and affairs of the church.[23]

A commitment to the complete lordship of Christ by an individual and the church can result in "no other sociological concept—the equality of every man before the Lord Christ and the elimination of all caste and class." James Mosteller notes that this principle is not always fully understood or even consistently practiced. The "democratic principle" is, however, universally accepted among Baptists. Congregational polity carries three implications for Mosteller.

First, the lordship of Christ as expressed in the democratic principle means that the individual believer is responsible for his direct call to and special service for ministry. Since Christ's lordship entails no human imposition between a person and God, the person is directly accountable to God for his own life and ministry. Second, the lordship of Christ as expressed in the democratic principle means that no distinctions between clergy and laity exist. The pastor and the layman share equally in the decisions regarding a local church. Third, the lordship of Christ as expressed in the democratic principle means that no church can exert authority or rank over another church. Churches share equally "mutual interdependence, voluntary cooperation, and spiritual unity" in organizations such as associations and conventions.[24]

Wayne Ward argues that Baptist churches endorse and practice congregational polity. Individual believers in Jesus Christ compose the church of Jesus Christ. As such, each and every member has an equal right and responsibility to express his understanding of the will of Christ for the congregation. This conviction is evidenced in all members participating in the calling of a pastor, the receiving of members, and the exercise of discipline. "Baptists insist that the whole congregation, as members of the body of Christ, must be involved in ascertaining and carrying out the word of her Lord." Baptist churches do not "set up a bishop or church hierarchy to mediate the authority of Christ."[25] Christ rules his church directly and personally through each individual believer.

Church polity should be "an example of true biblical democracy." This democracy is based upon the notion that each believer is a priest. As such, every priest is able to have direct access to God through Christ and is obligated to exercise his priestly gifts in the service of the local congregation. A local church is therefore a composition of priests forming a corporate priesthood functioning under the direct authority of Christ. "Baptist freedom does not in any way imply a personal anarchy or a congregational independence; to the contrary, it is a freedom jealously defended and carefully maintained in order to submit to an absolute monarchy, the lordship of Christ."

This priestly function compels each member of the church to participate equally in the ministries and decisions of the church. For Justice Anderson, clericalism is the antithesis of a biblical democracy. Although Baptist churches have formed associations or conventions of various types, these alliances in no way undermine the congregational autonomy of each church.[26]

Baptist polity is a Congregationalism in which God directly rules his people. Paul Beasley-Murray distinguishes between Congregationalism and democracy. Democracy emphasizes majority rule and should never be practiced in a Baptist church. Democracy can be conceived and executed without any intervention and involvement from God. Congregationalism is preferred because it requires the equal participation of the members and the guidance and involvement of the Holy Spirit in the process. Based upon this understanding, Beasley-Murray suggests that a Baptist church is a self-governing church in which all the members seek jointly and equally the will and guidance of God. Each local church is autonomous unto itself. No other ecclesiastical structure can impose authority upon a local church. Each local church functions ultimately under the lordship of Christ and may form "unions" for fellowship and for works of ministry too great for one local church.

Beasley-Murray also rejects clerical hierarchies. He notes that pastors in Baptist churches should have authority to lead. The authority to lead, however, does not imply a human imposition between an individual and God. The congregation willingly grants to the leadership pastoral authority. The laity are still bound to share equally in the decision-making processes of their church. Members do not capitulate their role to the pastor or bishop.[27]

SIGNIFICANCE

Baptist distinctives in the Reformation tradition attempt to implement a church polity based upon the New Testament. All within this tradition insist that the New Testament model is a congregational polity. Each member shares equally with the other members in the decisions and affairs of the church. The Scriptures prohibit hierarchical distinctions between the clergy and the laity. Each Baptist church is autonomous, and no church can exert ecclesiastical control or authority over another church.

The distinctive writings of the Enlightenment tradition share many common features with the Reformation tradition. All contend that a Baptist church should be self-governing through the members of the congregation. Each member is obligated to participate in the ministry and in the decision-making process within the church. All reject hierarchical clergy/laity distinctions and ecclesiastical control of one church by another.

One distinction, however, is identified between these two traditions of Baptist distinctives. The Reformation tradition is primarily concerned to construct a congregational model of polity based upon the New Testament. The ultimate concern is obedience to the Scriptures. Most writings in the Enlightenment tradition are more concerned to construct a congregational model of polity that protects and promotes the religious experience of the individual. The overall concern in this tradition is individual freedom and experience. This distinction is a further reflection of the different core distinctives of these two traditions.

CHAPTER EIGHT

A Distinctive Competency

....

The final component I want to examine is the volitional component. This element has two theological expressions: soul competency and religious freedom. As I mentioned earlier, these two concepts overlap in many areas of meaning. Whenever Baptists treat one of these issues, they typically discuss the other. Religious freedom implies individual soul competency, and soul competency leads naturally to discussions of religious liberty. Both ideas entail aspects of freedom and individuality.

Although both issues are intimately intertwined with each other, they are different ideas. I will therefore devote a chapter to each aspect of the volitional component. In the following survey, the reader will see the distinctive writings move back and forth between these two concepts. As we work through the materials, I will make every effort to keep these two notions as distinct as I possibly can. I cannot, however, completely prevent some overlap of discussion. The materials simply do not permit such neat separations.

The notion of soul competency as found in writings on Baptist distinctives contains several implications. It stipulates that every individual has the inherent capacity to seek and to obey God. Soul competency suggests the right and responsibility of every person to deal directly and personally with God without human imposition or interference of any kind. Further, it implies that an individual has the potential and the freedom to study and to obey the Scriptures to the best of his or her ability.

In a sense, soul competency offers the potential of the direct, immediate communion of the person with God. Every person has within himself a "secret place" in which God speaks to him or her and he or she in turn can potentially address God. Baptists argue that this concept is vital because the spiritual nature of the Christian faith mandates that each person deal directly with God. This process is uniquely individual. No other entity or person can participate in this personal encounter between God and the individual.

The essence of an individual's spiritual vitality, therefore, allows for no intrusions. Both the response of the individual and the proclamation of the gospel by the church are predicated upon the freedom and competency of the individual. Baptists oppose any attempts by any individual or group to impede or hinder the soul's right to commune with God.

SOUL COMPETENCY IN THE REFORMATION TRADITION

True religious reformation must include the idea the human soul has direct, unmediated access to God. Thus says John Quincy Adams. In his discussion of Baptist distinctives, Adams states that Baptists are the most thorough religious reformers because of the Baptist view of the "rights of conscience." He contends that every individual of the human race possesses the right "to think, and choose, and act for himself in religious matters." The right of conscience "acknowledges no human authority competent to come between the conscience and its Maker in reference to his will and its duty."

Adams asserts that this adherence to rights of conscience distinguishes Baptists from other Christian denominations. Even the Reformers of the Protestant Reformation disparaged the concept of the competency of the individual to deal directly with God without human imposition. The purest expression of soul competency for Adams is found in Baptist ecclesiology. The Baptist idea of the church, "composed of none but believers, immersed on their profession of faith," is the final expression of and necessary cause for the conception of liberty of conscience.[1]

Soul competency is best understood when discussed in conjunction with the nature of the church. J. M. Pendleton argues that the New Testament church is fundamentally a spiritual entity. The spiritual nature of a true church mandates that the spiritual rights of its members and the rights of those the church seeks to reach be protected from any human impositions. The Baptist appreciation for "soul-liberty is so great that they can allow no interference with it." They are categorically opposed to any entities or powers that seek "to intrude into the spiritual realm of conscience."[2]

Some Baptists derive the doctrine of soul competency from the doctrine of congregational church government. T. T. Eaton suggests that the distinctive view of Baptists regarding the nature of church polity carries implications for "soul liberty." All the members of a New Testament church are equal. Baptists "have ever insisted" that such a stipulation requires "soul liberty." Baptists "have ever resisted unto death the claims of any man or set of men to come between the individual soul and Christ. He and He alone is Lord of conscience." Eaton contends that this theological trait is distinctive only of Baptists.[3]

Baptist Why and Why Not understands soul competency as that which in part distinguishes Baptists from other Christian denominations. Because each person has an inherent ability to seek and to know God, Baptists believe that this ability should be cultivated and protected. "Baptists everywhere and always" have struggled "for independency, for the untrammeled rights of conscience." Soul competency therefore becomes that essential component that allows Baptists the freedom to obey biblical teachings, to construct a church composed of a regenerate church membership, and to implement congregational polity.[4]

Some Baptists understand soul competency as a natural derivation from the supreme authority of the Scriptures. Benjamin O. True argues that Baptists construct their churches in accordance with the teachings of the New Testament. Whereas other Protestant groups and the Roman Catholic church advocate the right of the state to interpret Scripture, Baptists teach the right of private interpretation and the right of the individual to obey the Scriptures according to conscience. Baptists conclude from this premise that "every man must have personal dealings with the Almighty." No external forces or structures should impede this inherent right of every person. True states that this view of the religious competency of the individual is true only of Baptists.[5]

Liberty of conscience, according to B. H. Carroll, is a necessary condition for the proper proclamation and reception of the gospel. This premise is found only among Baptists.

> The sole responsibility of decision and action rests directly on the individual. Each person must give account of himself to God. This is the first principle of New Testament law—to bring each "naked soul face to face with God." When that first Baptist voice broke the silence of four hundred years it startled the world with its appeal to individuality. Freedom of conscience dictates individual responsibility. "If one be responsible for himself, there must be not restraint or constraint of his conscience. Neither parent, nor government, nor church, may usurp the prerogative of God as Lord of the conscience. God himself does not coerce the will."

Carroll states that soul competency affects the membership, the polity, and the mission of a Baptist church. He further contends that freedom of conscience and the competency of the individual were virtually unknown until the rise of Baptists.[6]

Soul competency is the inalienable right of every person to worship God according to the dictates of his conscience and the right of free choice. According to W. R. White, this right is irrevocable and inviolate. God made man competent. This competency is not an "inherent qualification or merit, but is a divinely bestowed right based upon the mercy of God. Only God can bestow it, and only God can deprive him of it. And God will not remove it from him." Each person must inevitably deal directly and personally with the living God.

> Man must use his competency or misuse it. He must take the consequence of the choice, but no one can say him nay in the use of that right. Many may help or

hinder him. A large number may enter into his Christian experience at some point. But here comes a sacred moment and a holy place in the process when the individual must act independently, solitarily, and directly with his God. No man, however godly, and no angel, however exalted, can intervene as an intermediary at this solemn juncture.[7]

The soul's competency before God shapes the Baptist understanding of church membership and the relationships of believers within the overall corporate life of the church. White therefore indicates that the Baptist doctrine of the church is determined by and dependent upon the authority of the Scriptures and the competency of each individual before God.

Soul competency has been a part of Baptists almost from their inception. P. Lovene suggests that Baptists have always emphasized the inherent value and rights of the individual as to liberty of conscience. He defines liberty of conscience as every person's coming directly to God without human mediators. The idea of soul competency carries three implications. Soul competency suggests that individuals can enjoy personal, unmediated fellowship with God. Soul competency also entails the individual right of free access to the Bible and the right of private interpretation. Finally, soul competency undermines the distinction between clergy and laity and drives the church to practice congregational polity.[8]

The doctrine of soul competency underscores the spirituality of each individual. William Rone asserts that the New Testament teaches emphatically that "each soul is directly responsible to God and will eventually have to give an account to God." God has a divinely appointed medium through which the individual is to approach him. The teaching of the New Testament is that each soul is competent under God to approach him through the exclusive intermediary appointed by God in Christ. Soul competency carries two theological applications for Rone. Each person has liberty of conscience and competency of soul to pursue and to deal directly with God. Churches are also free to shape and structure their corporate worship and ministry in accordance with the teachings of the New Testament.[9]

For some Baptists soul competency is a defining trait of the essence of human nature. Henry Cook notes that the Christian religion rests "on the conviction that the individual soul is competent to deal directly with God, and has the right and the need of this direct dealing." To deny an individual the full exercise of this privilege is to deprive him of this most sacred right. To deprive a person of this right is to violate the dignity and worth of the individual as a human being. Coercion or restraint of the person's conscience is a sin against the individual, society, and God.

Cook further argues that soul competency is the basis of Christ's actions. Christ "could not force men to yield to His entreaties, for man, He knew, was free, and his freedom must be respected." Christ's callings and interactions with the people revolve around soul competency. The relationships within the corporate life of the church are directed by and built upon the freedoms of individuals joined together in the dynamic of Christian living and ministry. In a sense, the church is competent and free because it is comprised of individuals who are competent and free.[10]

Jack Hoad connects the corporate life of the church to the freedom and competency of the individual. The competency of the soul implies the ability of individuals to join together voluntarily for corporate worship and ministry in a church. Hoad states soul competency validates the sincerity of a church's membership and fellowship. Church members have the ability to decide whether they wish to join a church. They also have the freedom to assemble voluntarily with others who share similar theological convictions. Liberty of conscience is not a license for doctrinal laxity. Rather, liberty of conscience means that a local church has the right and the responsibility to discipline members who err doctrinally or live immorally.[11]

SOUL COMPETENCY IN THE ENLIGHTENMENT TRADITION

The Baptist identity is intertwined with soul competency. Walter Rauschenbusch argues that Baptists have always asserted that "a man may and must come into direct personal relations with God." All aspects of church life should be influenced and directed by the individual, personal experiences of its members. Since God created man free and competent, religious experience must be free and uncoerced. Although Baptists believe in confronting the soul with God, Baptists also trust in the inherent ability of the individual to discern and deal directly with God. Compulsion or coercion of faith has no spiritual value in the religious experience.[12]

Baptists have consistently and faithfully defended the inherent right and ability of each person to deal directly and personally with God. "In our postulate of soul-liberty we affirm the right of every human being to exemption in matters of faith and conscience from all coercion or intimidation by any earthly authority whatsoever." John Freeman states that this particular understanding of soul-liberty "inheres in the very essence" of the beliefs of Baptists. Baptists resist all attempts to coerce and manipulate faith within others. "Every attempt to put the conscience in thrall to human authority is *Lese-Majestev* to the King of kings, and a negation of the privileges and responsibilities conferred by Him upon the individual soul."[13]

E. Y. Mullins argues that the historical significance of Baptists, or that which is distinctively true of Baptists and not of other religious groups, is the competency of the soul. The doctrine of soul competency is a New Testament principle that carries "at its heart the very essence of that conception of man's relations to God." Soul competency is both exclusive and inclusive. It is exclusive in that it excludes all external "human interferences." These interferences include any understandings of faith as a "religion of proxy." Soul competency is inclusive in that it must entail the freedom of the individual to interact with God in order to fulfill "his religious destiny." Mullins views soul competency as a principle which "assumes that man is made in God's image, and that God is a person able to reveal himself to man, or Christian theism. Man has capacity for God, and God can communicate with man."[14]

The doctrine of an individual's right to have a relationship with God "has always been insisted upon by Baptists. Indeed, no doctrine has been, nor is, more Baptistic than this." Philip Jones states that Baptists are the teachers to the world of the "essentialness" and "worthiness" of this doctrine.[15]

> According to them [Baptists] the soul, as a unit, is answerable to God alone in the ultimate analysis. The man himself is competent in all religious matters, both for judgment and decision. So it comes about that the true Baptist is tolerant of others from the very nature of the case. What he claims for himself he accords to them.[16]

The Baptist doctrine of soul competency allows no imposition of any kind between the individual and God.

One of the significant meanings inherent within the experience of believer's baptism is the "right of the soul to an immediate relation to God." H. Wheeler Robinson contends that Baptists stand within the tradition of the Protestant

Reformation. As such, Baptists adhere to the doctrine of a universal priesthood for all believers. Intrinsic within this doctrinal position is the notion of a "prophetic consciousness" which "asserts that God could put aside all barriers and limits erected by human hands and reveal Himself to men, . . . and that man could approach God with the same simplicity and directness."

This "universal priesthood" for all believers implies the ability of the individual as well as the right and the desire of the person to have unhindered access to approach and to relate directly with the living God. "Any human priesthood is apt to seem an irrelevance, if not an impertinence, for those who have once experienced that fellowship in its direct simplicity."[17]

Christian experience as expressed in the competency of the soul of each person is the distinctive principle of Baptists. James Kirtley stipulates that "any person who ever lived or ever could live, has as much inherent right to deal personally with God as any other person who ever did or ever could live." Each human soul has as much right to have dealings with God as any other person. Kirtley provides four arguments to support his understanding.

First, all men were made in the one image of God. As such, all men possess within themselves equal rights. Second, all humanity shares a universal instinct of freedom. All persons feel the inherent right to be free. Third, all Christians share an instinct of fraternity toward all other believers. This fraternity instills a sense of family in all Christian relationships and a sense of equality with the family of God. Fourth, Jesus commanded all his followers to call no one Master except Christ. Since all family members are equal, the conclusion is that all Christians are to have personal dealings with God. In fact, all Christians have an obligation to relate directly to God. Baptists more than any other Christian denomination believe that "no man nor group of men can stand between any soul and God. . . . We say that only God can rule the soul, that he does so in Christ."[18]

In his polemic against Roman Catholic papal polity, James Rushbrooke says that each believer stands "in immediate relations" with the Lord. Each person is an equal in Christ with all other believers. Every believer enjoys equal and unhindered access to spiritual dealings with God. This unhindered access is innate within every individual and facilitates direct responsibility and the duty of private judgment.[19]

James Mosteller discusses soul competency within a broader discussion of freedom of conscience. Religion cannot be forced upon conscience by either civil or ecclesiastical authorities. "Baptists hold that religion is and must be perfectly voluntary, and that nothing except a voluntary surrender to Christ, and a voluntary service for Him, are acceptable." Mosteller equates the concepts of "soul competency," "soul liberty," and the "voluntary principle." All three concepts embody the implications that each man is free, spontaneous, able, and responsible to deal directly with God regarding matters of worship and conscience.[20]

In his broader discussion of religious liberty, Wayne Ward defines *soul competency* as "the competency of each individual soul to deal directly with God." He aligns soul competency so closely with religious freedom in his discussion that he seems to merge and use the terms interchangeably. With regard to soul competency and religious liberty, Ward states that neither civil nor ecclesiastical authorities can usurp the innate human responsibility or freedom. Ward's merger of these two conceptions can be seen in his view that religious freedom is the freedom and ability to believe in God or the freedom and ability to reject God. A true understanding of soul competency rests upon the freedom to reject or to accept God and his revelation.

If the Son of God "has made us free," then no legal or religious authority should dare impose a new slavery of creed, or tradition, or ritual. Religious liberty means the freedom to believe in God, or not to believe in God. It means the freedom to confess Christ as Lord, or not to confess Christ as Lord. It means the freedom to join his church, or not to join his church.[21]

The lordship of Christ implies the competency of each individual to deal directly with God. For Paul Beasley-Murray, Christ's lordship produces a priesthood of believers in which all human impositions between the individual and God are removed. Every person has the same opportunity and ability to deal personally with God. Likewise, each believer has an equal status and privilege before God. All believers should reflect the person of God to others and build bridges of reconciliation. Beasley-Murray derives soul competency from his understanding of the lordship of Christ and the priesthood of all believers.[22]

SIGNIFICANCE

The Reformation tradition shares many similarities with the Enlightenment tradition regarding soul competency. Both traditions maintain that Baptists originally developed and advocated soul competency and liberty of conscience. All the distinctive writings connect closely in some way soul competency and liberty of conscience. Soul competency is generally defined in the distinctive genre as the ability and right of each person to deal directly with God. Liberty of conscience addresses the freedom to participate or not to participate in such an endeavor. The importance of soul competency is an essential part of the overall Christian experience, which includes regeneration and Christian living.

The two traditions also have different emphases. The Reformation tradition normally emphasizes the importance of soul competency for Baptist ecclesiology. The ecclesiological doctrines addressed usually include issues such as church membership, polity, ministry, or the relationship of believers to one another. In the Enlightenment tradition, there are some implications of soul competency for Baptist ecclesiology. The primary thrust of these writings, however, is upon the significance of soul competency for the individual's religious experience. If I had to identify the major distinction between these two groups regarding soul competency, the difference would be the importance of soul competency for Baptist ecclesiology versus the importance of soul competency for understanding the nature of individual Christian experience.

For example, Baptists such as Adams, Pendleton, True, and F. Anderson, as well as treatises like *Baptist Why and Why Not,* develop the implications of soul competency for church membership. Others, such as Eaton and Lovene, investigate the significance of soul competency for church polity. Some, such as Carroll, examine the impact of soul competency upon church ministry, while others, like White, Rone, Cook, and Hoad, explore the influence that soul competency has upon the general Baptist understandings of church life.

CHAPTER NINE

A Distinctive Freedom

Most Protestant denominations today advocate in some form or another religious freedom. This has not always been the case. For centuries Baptists were the sole and foremost supporters of religious freedom. They have always stood for religious liberty. For them, acceptable worship and service of God must be unconstrained and voluntary. Otherwise, all religious disciplines are worthless.

As Baptists understand it, religious liberty is the right of each person to be free and uncoerced in his or her pursuit, or lack of pursuit, of a personal relationship with God. The theological traits that distinguished Baptists from other Christian denominations compel them to appeal uncompromisingly for the right of a free church in a free state. According to the Baptist position, no person should be constrained to become a church member who did not voluntarily accept Christ as Lord and who did not receive baptism willingly as a personal confession to this submission. Faith freely expressed and baptism personally affirmed are the necessary prerequisites for church membership. This understanding of the church and of Christian living is best realized within the context of religious freedom. As one prominent Baptist noted:

> Baptists . . . have been unswervingly loyal to the principle of religious liberty. Whatever may have been their faults . . . they have been free from the guilt of persecution. They have not only been the earnest advocates of religious liberty, but they have supported it in its fullest extent. They have not only claimed it for themselves, but have accorded it to others—Jews and pagans, as well as Christians.[1]

RELIGIOUS LIBERTY IN THE REFORMATION TRADITION

According to John Quincy Adams, Baptists more than any other religious group have propagated and defended religious liberty. He states that Baptists "stood alone, as the defenders of religious liberty, during the progress of the Reformation, and for many years after." Baptists oppose religious toleration, because toleration is not liberty. Baptists also view religious liberty as a theological corollary to soul competency.

> Religious freedom recognizes in no human organization the right or the power to tolerate. It does not stoop—either to magistrate or minister, pope or priest—to humbly ask

leave or beg permission to speak freely, or act out its convictions; but it speaks and acts because, in the exercise of its own right, it chooses to do so. . . . It acknowledges no human authority competent to come between the conscience and its Maker in reference to his will and its duty. Religious liberty does not exist where there is no recognition and acknowledgment of this right—the right of every individual of the human race, to think, and choose, and act for himself in religious matters.[2]

Baptists never force people "by legal enactments" to embrace or submit to a certain view. Baptists do not seek to unite the church with state, nor do they enforce any other religious teachings by force. Baptists refrain from all types of coercion to "force the conscience." These kinds of actions would violate the understanding of a regenerate church membership based upon a voluntary reception of the gospel of Christ.

Churches must be independent of the state. John Broadus asserts that the state should in no way violate the organization, faith, worship, and discipline of a church. Christians should be agreeable to the state and submit to it for just punishment if they violate laws that are beneficial to the order and welfare of society. The Baptist idea of the separation of church and state also prevents Christians from becoming dependent upon the state for monetary support.[3]

Baptists have always opposed the intrusion of the state in matters regarding the church. J. M. Pendleton notes that Baptists are friends of civil government and are supportive of civic leaders in their God-ordained duties to protect the innocent and prevent anarchy. They pray for their civic leaders, whether presidents or kings. Baptists, however, oppose the right of government to intrude into the realm of individual faith and conscience. A New Testament church is one that is founded, sustained, and promoted independently of and apart from the state.[4]

Baptists distinguish themselves from the Protestant Christians in their insistence that the church should remain independent from civic and ecclesiastical governments. According to *Baptist Why and Why Not,* the intrusion of government or church authority violates conscience and enslaves conviction. Whenever ecclesiastical or civic authorities exert inappropriate influence over the religious affairs of the church, widespread persecution results. The church also becomes carnal with the infusion of unregenerate persons into its membership. A New Testament church requires religious freedom in order to function according to the dictates of the consciences that form the membership of the church.[5]

Baptists believe no church should ever be united to any secular body or ecclesiastical hierarchy. B. H. Carroll argues that the state is a secular body that exists for secular purposes. It therefore can never be rightly joined to the church. Likewise, the church is a spiritual body that exists for spiritual purposes. It suffers irreparable injury when united with the state. Separation of the church from the state ensures that the church retains its ability to obey Christ. A church that is governed by any other structure except itself cannot have a pure and converted membership or ministry. A church that is joined to a state cannot speak against the sins of the state. Such unions place the church in financial dependence upon the government. In a sense, the state holds "the purse-strings" of the church.[6]

Baptists, more than any other Christian denomination, have always advocated religious freedom. W. R. White suggests that Baptists do not believe that religious freedom stifles or hinders their religious convictions. Rather, Baptists are willing to risk their message "before the bar of reason, conscience, spiritual consciousness, and the free choice of the individual." Baptists believe that is it within the forum of religious freedom that the religious experience of the individual and the ministry of the church are at their purest and truest expressions. The union of the church with the state destroys this religious freedom and taints the religious expression of the individual and the church with spiritual impurity. Church and state must always remain separate.

> There must be no union of church and state and no form of coercion in society in matters of faith. The union of church and state means either coercion or discriminatory advantages. Either is an enemy of freedom and equality. Every enemy of freedom and equality is an enemy of the primacy and dignity of the individual.[7]

Baptists believe that a church built after the New Testament sense functions best in an environment of religious freedom. In his discussion of religious liberty, P. Lovene states that a church in the New Testament sense is a spiritual and voluntary body of believers in Christ that exists for the purpose of leading people to and instructing them in the teachings of Christ. The church cannot and should not compel anyone to follow Christ by ecclesiastical or governmental force. Religious freedom protects individuals from external coercion and provides an environment for a free and unhindered response to the gospel. Christians should obey the state when the state does not demand obedience against the will of God. Lovene rejects the use of the powers of the state to coerce, correct, or influence matters of faith and practice in any respect.[8]

Religious freedom is one of Baptists' "noblest principles." Baptists have always insisted upon religious liberty. When the state and the church are kept separate, William Rone believes each entity conveys benefits to the others. A free church in a free society teaches its members respect for the dignity and value of human personality for themselves and others.

Religious freedom promotes sincerity, loyalty to God and country, high regard for one's neighbor, and a deep devotion to high ideals in life. A free church therefore promotes and produces excellent citizens. The government should provide the church with protection from evil and should ensure opportunity for matters of faith and practice.[9]

The most consistent and strongest support for religious freedom is an honor that belongs singularly to Baptists. Henry Cook stipulates that people must be free to decide for themselves their relation to God. Religious freedom implies the freedom to err in one's opinion of who God is and what God has done. This idea also helps protect the sincerity and acceptability of a person's devotion to God. Religious freedom involves risks. Cook believes that any dangers religious freedom might bring are far outweighed by the benefits for the spiritual experience of the individual and the vitality of the church. The New Testament serves as the foundation for and safeguard against the abuses of a religiously free society. Baptists therefore base their views of freedom upon the New Testament.[10]

RELIGIOUS FREEDOM IN THE ENLIGHTENMENT TRADITION

At a time when "the principle was novel and revolutionary," Baptists were the only religious group that insisted upon religious freedom. Walter Rauschenbusch claims that Baptist churches have always rejected the imposition of governmental authority or power in the spiritual affairs of the church. He discounts the claims of some Baptists who believe that the "secular realm" should be divorced from spiritual principles. Religious freedom as expressed in the true Baptist understanding suggests that the separation of church and state protects the church from the vested interests of the secular powers.

> Some Baptists seem to think that this separation is based
> on the idea that the spiritual life has nothing to do with
> the secular life. I utterly deny that assertion and think it
> is a calamitous heresy. Our Baptist forefathers insisted
> on that separation because they saw that it brought mis-
> chief when unspiritual men, actuated by political or
> covetous motives, tried to interfere with the centers of
> religious and moral life.[11]

The state benefits from this separation in that the political life
of a nation is free when questions of faith and practice are
removed from political debate.

The legacy of religious freedom is the lasting contribution
of Baptists to civil government. "The world must not be permitted to forget what the Baptist doctrine of soul-liberty,
broadening into the conception of personal liberty and finding
expression in the ordinances of civil liberty, has wrought for the
political emancipation of mankind." When the church and the
state are united, the result is a fruit "impoisonment and stung
with fire." John Freeman asserts: "Individuality in relation to
God and Christ and salvation, the Scriptures and judgment and
eternity, conducts by an irresistible sequence to freedom of
thought and speech and Press [sic], to popular government, to
unfettered scientific investigation, to universal education."[12]

Baptists have always opposed the "church state" as well as
the "state church." E. Y. Mullins states that the union of the
church to any authoritative structure results in the illegitimate
"absorption" of the church's spiritual energy. Soul competency
requires the exclusion of all human impositions between the
individual and God. The church must remain free from the
state and vice versa in order for God to deal directly and freely
with each individual. Mullins suggests that soul competency
demands "the doctrine of the separation of the Church and

State because State churches stand on the assumption that civil government is necessary as a factor in man's life in order to fulfill his religious destiny; that man without the aid of the State is incompetent in religion." Mullins rejects the necessity of such a union. He stipulates that without the separation of the church and state the freedom and competency necessary for individual religious experience are either diminished or destroyed.[13]

For Philip Jones, Baptists were the pioneers in the "severance of the Church and the State." "No student of history . . . can fail to discern this fact, that Baptists have been the pioneers in holding and defending that principle of the right relationship of Church and State which culminates in the ideal, a free Church in a free State." Religious liberty promotes the individual responsibility of each soul to deal directly with God. Religious liberty also promotes the direct, unmediated lordship of Christ in each believer's life. This religious liberty must be granted to all persons in order that they may pursue and accept or reject the gospel call of God.[14]

Liberty, however, must also be shaped and limited. For George Horr, religious liberty has limitations. As a lone theological principle, religious freedom is insufficient to provide unity. Religious liberty is rather "limited by the general position" or the principles of the church with which a person unites. Furthermore, once a relationship has been established, liberty is in some measure limited. "We part with some share of our liberty whenever we cooperate with others. . . . The unifying tie in all these relationships is not liberty, but the agreement of ideals, which constitute the reason for the existence of the organization."[15]

The passion of Baptists for liberty is one of their most strongly marked characteristics, flowing directly from their primary emphasis of spiritual individualism. H. Wheeler Robinson demonstrates through a historical survey of prominent Baptist leaders that Baptists were "the first to claim and the first to apply fearlessly the unfettered principle of freedom for religion." He defines two types of religious freedom.

The first type is an external freedom. External religious freedom is the removal of governmental or ecclesiastical intrusion into the individual's spiritual pilgrimage and spiritual dealings with God. The second type of religious freedom is internal religious freedom, which is much more difficult to achieve. This freedom is the removal of all prejudices within the human heart. Prejudices are more subtle and dangerous than any other impediment to freedom. Only through the process of personal religious experience can a person attain internal freedom.[16]

One major threat to the exercise of the competency of the soul in religious matters is the union of the church and the state. James Kirtley asserts that state churches are "monstrosities" because they pervert the power of the government and assault the power of choice. The existence of such entities results in the suppression of an individual's God-given right to deal directly with God as led by the Spirit of God. Kirtley concludes that the doctrine of the separation of church and state and the resulting idea of religious freedom is distinctive only of Baptists.[17]

Some Baptists, such as James Mosteller, see three aspects to the Baptist understanding of religious freedom. First, religious liberty is freedom of worship. This means "that every person must be guaranteed the right to go to the church of his choice freely and without interference . . . and to worship according to the dictates of his own conscience." Second, religious liberty is the freedom of conscience. This understanding presumes that there "must be no forcing of the conscience in matters of religion, either by an ecclesiastical or civil authority." Religion must be perfectly voluntary both in surrender to Christ and in service for him. Third, religious liberty mandates the freedom of witness. Freedom of witness is the God-given right to propagate the faith.[18]

Mosteller separates the notions of religious liberty and the separation of church and state. For him, religious liberty is a spiritual issue for church life and ministry. This kind of freedom can be guaranteed only by the existence of the supporting principle in the political sphere, the separation of church and state.

Religious liberty is basic to the distinctive theological identity of Baptists. Religious liberty, according to Wayne Ward, is not to be equated with the separation of church and state. The separation of church and state is purely a political connotation. He argues that religious liberty transcends political connotations. Religious liberty "is basic to every other liberty. A man's religion is his ultimate belief, his absolutely basic assumption about the nature of reality and the meaning of the universe." Religious liberty entails the freedom to pursue one's "ultimate belief" and the protection from all external forces that would impede or hinder this pursuit.[19]

Baptists are the religious group that first introduced religious freedom into Christianity. Norman Cavendar notes that Baptist history is "rich with commitment to the full separation of church and state." Baptists teach that government should not be allowed to involve itself in any way with the proclamation and ministry of the church. Secular, human government cannot substitute for God. If a church becomes entangled with the state, the government will invariably favor one denomination over another or will coerce or suppress certain religious convictions or practices. "Thus government separates from faith, and leaves it to the various faiths—and to the power of faith—to prevail. . . . In matters of faith, government is non-partisan and must always be non-partisan." Cavendar contends that the Christian gospel is best served when full liberty is guaranteed. This understanding is part of the distinctive identity of the Baptists.[20]

SIGNIFICANCE

The Reformation tradition and the Enlightenment tradition share many similarities regarding religious freedom. All these writings maintain that Baptists were the first and foremost proponents of this position. All stipulate that religious freedom is a necessary corollary to soul competency. The necessity of religious freedom ensures a converted, voluntary church membership. All agree that religious liberty is best expressed politically in the separation of church and state. The distinctive genre views the state as having a necessary and appropriate place in God's purposes. Equally important is the shared concern of Baptists to oppose ecclesiastical as well as political intrusion into the spiritual affairs of the individual and of the church. Religious freedom promotes equality between individual believers and between churches. The goal of religious freedom in Baptist thought is an individual's genuine and sincere religious experience. Religious freedom not only benefits the church but it also benefits the state.

Differences between the two traditions of Baptist distinctives do exist. These are minimal and are more a matter of emphasis than major doctrinal content. The Reformation tradition understands religious freedom both in terms of individual benefit and in terms of benefit to the church. Religious liberty in these writings has strong overtones for the nature and function of the church. Strands of such ideas can be found in the Enlightenment tradition. The corporate emphasis is more diminished in this tradition than in the Reformation tradition. The primary emphasis in the Enlightenment tradition is more upon the personal benefits and implications for an individual than upon the corporate benefits to the church.

Conclusion:
Distinctively Baptist

· ·

In this final chapter, I want to consider two additional issues on the subject of Baptist distinctives. First, I will examine the subject of the "absoluteness" or the "relativity" of Baptist distinctives. Are Baptist distinctives peculiar only to Baptists, or are these theological traits found in other Christian denominations? If these tenets are found in other Christian denominations, can they truly be regarded as "baptistic?" After this, I will propose what I consider the authentic Baptist distinctive tradition.

BAPTIST DISTINCTIVES:
ABSOLUTE OR RELATIVE?

Are Baptist distinctives relative, or are they absolute? The relativity of Baptist distinctives is the idea that Baptist distinctives are only distinctive when they are compared to other Christian denominations. The absoluteness of Baptist distinctives is the notion that Baptist distinctives are absolutely distinctive in comparison with other Christian denominations; that is, Baptist distinctives are true only of Baptists.

The evidence convinces me that Baptist distinctives are "absolute." One Baptist theologian has noted that other Christian groups can and do adopt Baptist distinctives. When a person or group incorporates these distinctives into their denominational identity, the principles are still "baptistic."[1] This perspective interprets the distinctive theological components of Baptists as absolute to Baptists. When the theological tenets identified in this study exist in other Christian groups, the doctrinal tenets should still be regarded as "Baptist."

Several reasons support this position. First, Baptist history reveals that the peculiar theological identity of Baptists did not exist before the rise of Baptists. If Baptist distinctives existed in other Christian denominations, then logic suggests that the development of Baptist distinctives was a duplication of an already existing group of beliefs. History indicates that no Christian group existed that shared or articulated the distinctive theological concerns of Baptists. This absence naturally leads to the conclusion that Baptist distinctives did not exist until the rise of Baptists.

Another consideration supporting the absolute nature of Baptist distinctives is found within the distinctive writings themselves. The presence of the polemical component suggests that Baptists believed that their unique theological tenets were absent in other Christian denominations. The existence of the polemical component insinuates that the formulators of Baptist distinctives did not see the epistemological, ecclesiological, and volitional components in other Christian groups as understood by Baptists. Distinctive writings contend that the unique presence and the arrangement of the previously identified components were true only of Baptists. The polemical component within writings on Baptist distinctives therefore argues for an absoluteness to Baptist distinctives.

A third consideration is the perspective of non-Baptist Christians. Various Christian individuals and denominations have often questioned and challenged the existence and theological distinctives of the Baptists. Writings on Baptist distinctives were often produced to address the challenges posed by these various entities. For example, R. M. Dudley recounts a challenge given by a Dr. Jessup, moderator of the Presbyterian General Assembly, during a celebration of the anniversary of the Northern Baptist societies in 1879 in Saratoga, New York. During the meeting, Jessup challenged the Baptists to provide "adequate reasoning for the separate existence of Baptists as a denomination."

Dudley's development of Baptist distinctives was his answer to Jessup's inquiry to justify the existence of Baptists. Dudley's goal was to establish the credibility and viability of the Baptists and their distinctive theological tenets. He argued that Baptists exist because their unique theological doctrines were not found in any other Christian denomination.[2]

The adoption of the theological tenets identified as Baptist distinctives by non-Baptist denominations does not diminish the "baptisticness" of such doctrines. Christian denominations or groups that embrace these principles can be considered "baptistic" to the degree that they affirm these concepts. The quest of many authors of Baptist distinctives was to convince non-Baptist Christians to adopt Baptist distinctives (i.e., Adams, Broadus, Pendleton, Kirtley, Rone, and Hoad). These writings state that non-Baptist groups ought to embrace Baptist distinctives. The rationale frequently followed was that true ecumenicity would exist only when all Christians appropriate Baptist distinctives. The presence of Baptist distinctives among non-Baptist Christians did not undermine the absolute nature of these distinctives but rather served the ultimate purpose for which many of these writings were produced.

If Baptist distinctives are "absolute," how then do we explain their presence in some non-Baptist groups? Many groups that have adopted Baptist distinctives within their confessional traditions are part of the modern evangelical movement. Millard J. Erickson points out that many of the early organizers and participants of this movement were Baptists, among whom are Carl F. H. Henry, Billy Graham, Edward J. Carnell, and Bernard Ramm.[3] One plausible explanation could be that these and other individuals infused many of the Baptist distinctives into the modern evangelical movement. Hence, many non-Baptist evangelical denominations contain some of the Baptist distinctives.

Are there any non-Baptist Christian denominations that advocate all the theological distinctives of Baptists? Can a Christian denomination embrace all the theological tenets defined as Baptist distinctives and not be Baptist? In my judgment, the answer is no. Although many groups may adopt some of the distinctive theological tenets of Baptists, no denomination affirms all the Baptist distinctives completely. For example, the Disciples of Christ and the Churches of Christ affirm baptism by immersion. Yet, these denominations do not share the Baptist understanding of the meaning of baptism. Also, many Bible churches advocate local church autonomy and religious freedom. Most of these churches, however, differ from Baptists in their view of church polity and mode of baptism.

No Christian denomination appears to embrace consistently all the distinctive theological traits of Baptists in the same manner as Baptists. On the basis of the material examined, Baptist distinctives in their entirety should be regarded as "absolute" to Baptists.

WHICH TRADITION IS CORRECT?

Having completed my analysis, I now want to make my own contribution to the discussion. What are Baptist distinctives? Or, more correctly, which of the two Baptist distinctive traditions is correct? Which tradition best reflects the historical and theological tenets that have always been true of Baptists and has given them their distinctive theological identity? On the basis of all the materials and evidence presented, I believe that the Reformation tradition best embodies what it means to be distinctively Baptist.

The early Baptists who first formulated the distinctive genre considered their existence the logical outcome of the ideas of the Reformation. They particularly believed that Baptists consistently represented the notion of what it means to construct a church and Christian beliefs supremely and uniquely on the Bible. The concern for absolute submission to biblical authority was the passion of early Baptists. This conviction is what led them to separate from other Christian denominations.

If the early Baptists perceived that another Christian group embodied an understanding of biblical authority as they understood the concept, they probably would have joined that group. Instead, these individuals felt constrained to remove themselves from existing Christian denominations in order to submit themselves to biblical authority as they understood it. The rise

of Baptists in history makes no sense if we discount the pro-
found commitment these individuals had to biblical authority.
It was this commitment to biblical authority that the early
Baptists believed distinguished them from other Christian
denominations. Any accurate assessment of Baptist distinctives
must in some form or another account for this high view of the
place of the Bible for constructing faith and practice.

In light of this, should Baptists affirm the entire Bible or
only the New Testament as their final authority? It seems to me
that asking this question in isolation from other considerations
is rather superficial. Part of the answer must be determined by
the particular theological issues under consideration. Most
Baptists in one form or another recognize the inspiration and
authority of both Old and New Testaments. Such doctrines as
the nature and personhood of God, the doctrine of creation, or
the doctrine of sin and the fall of humanity, for example,
require the authoritative and inspired voice of the Old
Testament for theological construction. No Baptist, past or
present, would ever discount the value and place of the Old
Testament as revelation from God, its vital place in the biblical
canon, and its necessity for theological construction. The Old
Testament must be used for the doctrinal development of many
beliefs that are crucial to the Christian faith.

If, however, the doctrine under consideration is the nature
and purpose of the church, then the New Testament certainly
provides fuller and clearer revelation on the matter. Baptists do
recognize the progressive nature of revelation. Progressive revelation is the notion that later revelation builds upon and
expands previous revelation. The New Testament provides revelation on the distinctive traits of Baptists that are not fully
developed or revealed in the Old Testament. In this sense, the
New Testament supplies and fulfills what is lacking or unclear
in the Old Testament. A regenerate church membership, the

ordinances, church polity, and other like doctrines are best constructed and interpreted from the New Testament. As Baptists, we construct our doctrine of the church primarily from the New Testament.

Some early Baptists objected strongly to constructing the doctrine of the church upon the Old Testament. Many of their Christian contemporaries developed their understanding of the nature and purpose of the church primarily from Old Testament texts. Baptists pointed out that much of the theological rationale for state-established churches and infant baptism was based upon Old Testament passages at the exclusion of the New Testament. The doctrine of a New Testament church for these non-Baptist denominations was built upon Old Testament passages. Baptists rejected this method outright. This perspective helps explain in part why some Baptists were so adamant in using only the New Testament to develop the doctrine of the church.

We would do well to remember and receive the lessons these early Baptists learned. I would concur with the notion that, by and large, our understanding of the church comes primarily from the New Testament. Most of the distinctive theological identity of Baptists is enmeshed in their doctrine of the church. This affirmation does not, however, exclude or diminish the value of the Old Testament for other doctrinal formulations. With these qualifications in mind, it seems appropriate to say that Baptists find their distinctive theological identity primarily in the New Testament.

Baptists best express their distinctive commitment to biblical authority in the way they do church. The doctrines of a regenerate church, the ordinances, and church polity are, as we have seen, attempts to have a church established on the authority of God as expressed in the Bible, not on the authority of men as expressed in human traditions. Baptist distinctives developed in part as a reaction against Christian denominations that Baptists felt were not seeking pure churches composed only of those who have testified to a regenerating work of God. Baptists have always been concerned that the church should reflect God's intentions as closely as possible. Thus, the Baptist understanding of the church is the attempt of Baptists to reflect their obedience and submission to biblical authority. To put it another way, a Baptist church manifests visibly the Reformation premise of *sola scriptura*.

The volitional component is derived from biblical authority and a New Testament church. Religious freedom and soul competency are doctrinal corollaries. These tenets are essential in order to have a regenerate church that conforms to biblical teachings. Soul competency and religious freedom should be subordinated to the doctrine of the church. The Enlightenment tradition, in my opinion, reverses the order. In this tradition, the tenets of soul competency and religious freedom precede the nature and purpose of the church. The result of this method is a church that exists to sustain and promote individual freedom and autonomy. This does not represent accurately the biblical witness or Baptist theology. The early Baptists pursued religious freedom in order to have a church based upon and submitted to biblical authority.

The method for constructing Baptist distinctives, then, is to begin with biblical authority. The Bible is the basis for all theological claims. This is the first and most basic presupposition of Baptist distinctives. The second step is to build a doctrine of the church upon this foundation. Baptists develop their ecclesiology as closely as possible on the teachings of the New Testament. The doctrines that are most visibly affected by this commitment in the Baptist confessional tradition are the doctrines of a regenerate church, believer's baptism, and congregational church polity. These doctrines best embody the thoroughgoing commitment of Baptists to biblical authority.

The third step is the construction of the volitional component. In order to have a New Testament church that reflects an unequivocal commitment to the Bible, Baptists contend for a free church in a free society. Religious freedom helps ensure the authenticity of the conversion experience and protects the voluntary nature of a free church. Soul competency stipulates the prerogative and responsibility of every person to give an account of his or her own life to God. The genuineness of this accounting must occur in a context that removes spiritual coercion and religious manipulation.

Both religious freedom and soul competency promote the purity of a church built upon the conviction that the Bible is the absolute authority for faith and practice. The Reformation tradition of Baptist distinctives best embodies these ideals. In light of the evidence, this is what I believe makes a Baptist a Baptist.

THE FINAL WORD?

Two challenges face Baptists today. One is to be faithful to the heritage that is uniquely Baptist. Those who claim the name *Baptist* have a rich theological history. Part of our Baptist identity are those tenets that we share with all Christians. Baptists should recognize that they are one part of God's overall kingdom work. As such, they should seek any and every opportunity to join together in God's kingdom work with those who believe in the great truths of the Christian faith. Part of our heritage also are those truths that define us as Baptists. We must appreciate the unique identity forged by those who discovered and refined these distinctives. As Baptists, we have an obligation to represent accurately and faithfully our confessional tradition. To misrepresent or modify the tenets that have historically represented the distinctive theological identity of Baptists is to belittle the labor and sacrifice of those who have gone before us.

The second challenge before modern Baptists is the task of articulating our distinctive identity to our contemporary culture. This must be done with care and caution. On the one hand, if we are not careful, we can so accommodate our distinctives to current theological trends that we change the essence of the Baptist confessional tradition. On the other hand, if we are not sensitive to culture concerns, we run the risk of preserving our distinctives in such a way that they are unintelligible to a contemporary audience. The present culture will neither understand nor appreciate the contribution that Baptist distinctives can make to current ministry and church concerns. As our Baptist ancestors have taught us, our Baptist distinctives can do both. They can embody faithfully the great truths that have shaped us as a part of God's kingdom people. They are dynamic enough that they can speak to any contemporary context and do so in a way that engages thoughtfully and critically the theological concerns of time.

The distinctive theology of Baptists is still greatly needed today. It remains to be seen whether Baptists will rise to the occasion to reclaim their theological heritage in order to shape ministry and engage a culture that is both sophisticated and contemporary yet ancient and pagan. Only time will tell if the people distinctively called Baptists are up to the challenge.

Notes

CHAPTER 1, DEFINING BAPTIST DISTINCTIVE GENRE

1. John Quincy Adams, *Baptists the Only Thorough Religious Reformers*, rev. ed. (New York: Sheldon & Co., 1876), 162.
2. Henry Cook, *What Baptists Stand For* (London: Kingsgate Press, 1947), 18.
3. B. H. Carroll, *Baptists and Their Doctrines; Sermons on Distinctive Baptist Principles*, comp. by J. B. Cranfill (Chicago: F. H. Revell Co., 1913), 11.
4. J. M. Pendleton, *Three Reasons Why I Am a Baptist; With a Fourth Reason Added on Communion*, 13th ed. (Nashville: Graves, Marks, and Rutland, 1856), 5–6.
5. Timothy George, *Baptist Confessions, Covenants, and Catechism* (Nashville: Broadman & Holman, 1996), 2–4.
6. E. Y. Mullins, *The Axioms of Religion: A New Interpretation of the Baptist Faith* (Philadelphia: Griffith & Rowland, 1908), 59–69.
7. For a resource that exceptionally illustrates this component, see T. T. Eaton in *Baptist Why and Why Not* (Nashville: Sunday School Board of the Southern Baptist Convention, 1900).
8. Pendleton, *Three Reasons Why I Am a Baptist*, 32–137.

9. T. T. Eaton, *The Faith of Baptists* (Louisville: Baptist Book Concern, 1903), 20–41.

10. Henry Cook, *What Baptists Stand For*, 17, 32.

11. H. Wheeler Robinson, *The Life and Faith of the Baptists* (London: Kingsgate Press, 1946), 97–110.

12. Mullins, *The Axioms of Religion*, 150–57.

13. Eric H. Ohlmann, "The Essence of the Baptists: A Reexamination," *Perspectives in Religious Studies* 13 (Fall 1986): 87.

14. Walter Rauschenbusch, *Why I Am a Baptist* (Philadelphia: Baptist Leader, 1958), in *Rochester Baptist Monthly* 20 (1905–06), 3.

15. D. L. Baker, "Biblical Theology," in *New Dictionary of Theology*, eds. Sinclair B. Ferguson, David F. Wright, and J. I. Packer (Downers Grove: InterVarsity Press, 1988), 96–99.

16. James Leo Garrett Jr., *Systematic Theology*, vol. 1 (Grand Rapids: Wm. B. Eerdmans, 1990), 54.

17. Colin Brown, "Philosophical Theology," in *New Dictionary of Theology*, 510–11.

18. James Leo Garrett Jr., "The History of Christian Doctrine: Retrospect and Prospect," *Review and Expositor* 58 (Spring 1971): 259.

19. George, *Baptist Confessions*, 1–5.

20. Alan Richardson, "Confession(s), Confessionalism," in *The Westminster Dictionary of Christian Theology*, ed., Alan Richardson and John Bowden (Philadelphia: Westminster Press, 1983), 116–17.

21. Martin Cook, *The Open Circle* (Minneapolis: Fortress Press, 1991), 2–3.

CHAPTER 2, FORMATION OF DOCTRINE

1. One scholar who denies the presence of one core distinctive as an organizing principle for the other distinctives is Eric H. Ohlmann, "The Essence of the Baptists: A Reexamination," *Perspectives in Religious Studies* 13 (Fall 1986): 83–104.

2. James Leo Garrett Jr., "Major Emphases in Baptist Theology," *Southwestern Journal of Theology* 37 (Summer 1995): 44.

3. T. T. Eaton, *The Faith of Baptists* (Louisville: Baptist Book Concern, 1903), 3–19.

4. Norman H. Maring and Winthrop S. Hudson, *A Baptist*

Manual of Polity and Practice (Chicago: Judson Press, 1963), 15, 17–32.

5. J. R. Graves, *Old Landmarkism: What Is It?* 2nd ed. (Memphis: Baptist Book House, 1881), 35–52.

6. J. M. Pendleton, *Distinctive Principles of Baptists* (Philadelphia: American Baptist Publication Society, 1882), 90–158.

7. James Henry Rushbrooke, *Protestant of the Protestants: The Baptist Churches, Their Progress, and Their Spiritual Principle* (London: Kingsgate Press, 1926), 70–71.

8. G. Thomas Halbrooke, "Why I Am a Baptist," in *Being Baptist Means Freedom,* ed. Alan Neely (Charlotte, N.C.: Southern Baptist Alliance, 1988), 3–5.

9. H. Wheeler Robinson, *The Life and Faith of Baptists,* (London: Kingsgate Press, 1946), 11.

10. Ibid.

11. Robinson, *Baptist Principles,* 4th ed. (London: Kingsgate Press, 1966), 23.

12. John D. Freeman, "The Place of Baptists in the Christian Church," in *Baptist World Congress, London, July 11–19, 1905. Authorised Record of Proceedings* (London: Baptist Union Publication Department, 1905), 22.

13. James D. Mosteller, "Basic Baptist Principles and the Contemporary Scene," *Southwestern Journal of Theology* 6 (April 1964): 60–81.

14. Ibid., 62.

15. T. T. Eaton, *Baptist Why and Why Not* (Nashville: Sunday School Board of the Southern Baptist Convention, 1900), 45.

16. William H. Rone, *The Baptist Faith and Roman Catholicism,* rev. ed. (Kingsport, Tenn.: Kingsport Press, 1952), 3.

17. Walter Rauschenbusch, *Why I Am a Baptist* (Philadelphia: Baptist Leader, 1958), in *Rochester Baptist Monthly* 20 (1905–06), 2.

18. S. F. Skevington, *The Distinctive Principles of the Baptists* (printed for private distribution, 1914), 9–10.

19. Wayne E. Ward, "What Is a Baptist? Personal Religious Freedom," *Western Recorder,* 4 April, 1970, 2.

CHAPTER 3, A NEW DISTINCTIVE TRADITION

1. Herschel H. Hobbs, *The Axioms of Religion,* rev. ed. (Nashville: Broadman Press, 1978).

2. E. Y. Mullins, *Freedom and Authority in Religion* (Philadelphia: Griffith & Rowland Press, 1913), 151–54.

3. Mullins, *The Christian Religion in Its Doctrinal Expression* (Boston: Judson Press, 1917), 61, 112.
4. Mullins, *Freedom and Authority in Religion*, 122–23, 151–53.
5. Mullins, *The Christian Religion in Its Doctrinal Expression*, 49–50.
6. Mullins, *Why Is Christianity True?* (Philadelphia: American Baptist Publication Society, 1905), 266.
7. Mullins, *The Christian Religion in Its Doctrinal Expression*, 41.
8. Ibid., 67–68.
9. Ibid., 8–10.
10. Mullins, *The Christian Religion in Its Doctrinal Expression*, 56.
11. Mullins, *The Axioms of Religion: A New Interpretation of the Baptist Faith* (Philadelphia: Griffith & Rowland, 1908), 59–69.
12. Mullins, *Why Is Christianity True?*, 17.

CHAPTER 4, A DISTINCTIVE AUTHORITY

1. John Quincy Adams, *Baptists the Only Thorough Religious Reformers*, rev. ed. (New York: Sheldon & Co., 1876), 22–23, 47–48, 53–55.
2. T. T. Eaton, *Baptist Why and Why Not* (Nashville: Sunday School Board of the Southern Baptist Convention, 1900), 12–14.
3. Ibid., 28–30.
4. J. M. Pendleton, *Distinctive Baptist Principles* (Philadelphia: American Baptist Publication Society, 1882), 11–13.
5. J. B. Gambrell and others, *Baptist Principles Reset, Consisting of a Series of Articles on Distinctive Baptist Principles*, 3rd ed. (Richmond, Va.: Religious Herald, 1902), 252.
6. W. R. White, *Baptist Distinctives* (Nashville: Sunday School Board of the Southern Baptist Convention, 1946), 1–7.
7. Jack Hoad, *The Baptist: An Historical and Theological Study of the Baptist Identity* (London: Grace Publications Trust, 1986), 14–15.
8. John A. Broadus, *The Duty of Baptists to Teach Their Distinctive Views* (Philadelphia: American Baptist Publication Society, 1881), 6–11.
9. P. Lovene, *Distinctive Baptist Principles*, 2nd ed. rev. (Chicago: Baptist Conference Press, 1950), 12–13.
10. B. H. Carroll, *Baptists and Their Doctrines; Sermons on Distinctive Baptist Principles*, comp. J. B. Cranfill (Chicago: F. H. Revell Co., 1913), 10–11.

11. Henry Cook, *What Baptists Stand For* (London: Kingsgate Press, 1947), 18–19, 31.
12. Robert A. Baker, *The Baptist March in History* (Nashville: Convention Press, 1958), 1–11.
13. Winthrop S. Hudson, *Baptist Convictions* (Valley Forge, Pa.: Judson Press, 1963), 6–7.
14. Mullins, *Axioms of Religion*, 26–30, 131, 143.
15. H. Wheeler Robinson, *The Life and Faith of Baptists* (London: Kingsgate Press, 1966), 7–8, 15–18.
16. Walter Rauschenbusch, *Why I Am a Baptist* (Philadelphia: Baptist Leader, 1958), in *Rochester Baptist Monthly* 20 (1905–06), 2, 9.
17. George Edwin Horr, *The Baptist Heritage* (Philadelphia: Judson Press, 1923), 86–90.
18. Cecil Sherman, "Freedom of the Individual to Interpret the Bible," in *Being Baptist Means Freedom*, ed. Alan Neely (Charlotte, N.C.: Southern Baptist Alliance, 1988), 12–16, 24.
19. John D. Freeman, "The Place of Baptists in the Christian Church," in *Baptist World Congress, London, July 11–19, 1905. Authorised Record of Proceedings* (London: Baptist Union Publication Department, 1905), 22–29.
20. Wayne E. Ward, "Who Is a Baptist? The Authority of the Bible," in *Western Recorder*, 11 April 1970, 2.
21. James D. Mosteller, "Basic Baptist Principles and the Contemporary Scene," *Southwestern Journal of Theology* 6 (April 1964): 63–65.

CHAPTER 5, A DISTINCTIVE CHURCH

1. John Quincy Adams, *Baptists the Only Thorough Religious Reformers*, rev. ed. (New York: Sheldon & Co., 1876), 81–83, 97, 150.
2. John A. Broadus, *The Duty of Baptists to Teach Their Distinctive Views* (Philadelphia: American Baptist Publication Society, 1881), 6–7.
3. J. M. Pendleton, *Distinctive Baptist Principles* (Philadelphia: American Baptist Publication Society, 1882), 159–60.
4. Ibid., 168.
5. J. B. Jeter, *Baptist Principles Reset, Consisting of a Series of Articles on Distinctive Baptist Principles*, 3rd ed. (Richmond, Va.: Religious Herald, 1902), 26, 55–56.
6. Alvah Hovey, *Baptist Principles Reset*, 150.
7. B. H. Carroll, *Baptists and Their Doctrines; Sermons on*

Distinctive Baptist Principles, comp. by J. B. Cranfill (Chicago: F. H. Revell Co., 1913), 22–23.

8. George W. McDaniel, *The People Called Baptists* (Nashville: Sunday School Board of the Southern Baptist Convetion, 1919), 52.

9. Ibid., 54–55.

10. W. R. White, *Baptist Distinctives* (Nashville: Sunday School Board of the Southern Baptist Convention, 1946), 37.

11. Herbert Gezork, "Our Baptist Faith in the Word To-Day," in *Baptist World Alliance Golden Jubilee Congress, London, 1955* (London: Carey Kingsgate Press, 1955), 42–44.

12. Henry Cook, *What Baptists Stand For* (London: Kingsgate Press, 1947), 51.

13. Jack Hoad, *The Baptist: An Historical and Theological Study of the Baptist Identity* (London: Grace Publications Trust, 1986), 16.

14. Walter Rauschenbusch, *Why I Am a Baptist* (Philadelphia: Baptist Leader, 1958), in *Rochester Baptist Monthly* 20 (1905–06), 2.

15. John D. Freeman, "The Place of Baptists in the Christian Church," in *Baptist World Congress, London, July 11–19, 1905. Authorised Record of Proceedings* (London: Baptist Union Publication Department, 1905), 27–28.

16. E. Y. Mullins, *The Axioms of Religion: A New Interpretation of the Baptist Faith* (Philadelphia: Griffith & Rowland, 1908), 107–26, 132–35.

17. Philip Jones, *A Restatement of Baptist Principles* (Philadelphia: Griffith & Rowland Press, 1909), 44–45.

18. James Kirtley, *The Baptist Distinctive and Objective* (Philadelphia: Judson Press, 1926), 10–21.

19. George Edwin Horr, *The Baptist Heritage* (Philadelphia: Judson Press, 1923), 88–90.

20. H. Wheeler Robinson, *The Life and Faith of Baptists* (London: Kingsgate Press, 1966), 17.

21. James Henry Rushbrooke, *Protestant of the Protestants: The Baptist Churches, Their Progress, and Their Spiritual Principle* (London: Kingsgate Press, 1926), 70, 75, 79.

22. James D. Mosteller, "Basic Baptist Principles and the Contemporary Scene," *Southwestern Journal of Theology* 6 (April 1964): 65–66.

23. Wayne E. Ward, "Who Is a Baptist? Personal Regeneration and Faith," *Western Recorder* 18 (April 1970): 2.

24. Justice C. Anderson, "Old Baptist Principles Reset," *Southwestern Journal of Theology* 31 (Spring 1989): 8.

CHAPTER 6, A DISTINCTIVE ORDINANCE

1. John Quincy Adams, *Baptists the Only Thorough Religious Reformers*, rev. ed. (New York: Sheldon & Co., 1876), 150–52.
2. John A. Broadus, *The Duty of Baptists to Teach Their Distinctive Views* (Philadelphia: American Baptist Publication Society, 1881), 8.
3. J. M. Pendleton, *Distinctive Baptist Principles* (Philadelphia: American Baptist Publication Society, 1882), 120–21.
4. Ibid., 170–71.
5. T. T. Eaton, *The Faith of Baptists* (Louisville: Baptist Book Concern, 1903), 15, 20, 55.
6. *Baptist Why and Why Not* (Nashville: Sunday School Board of the Southern Baptist Convention, 1900), 30–32, 183–84.
7. J. B. Jeter, *Baptist Principles Reset, Consisting of a Series of Articles on Distinctive Baptist Principles*, 3rd ed. (Richmond, Va.: Religious Herald, 1902), 26, 55–56.
8. Ibid., 64–68.
9. B. H. Carroll, *Baptists and Their Doctrines; Sermons on Distinctive Baptist Principles*, comp. by J. B. Cranfill (Chicago: F. H. Revell Co., 1913), 33.
10. George W. McDaniel, *The People Called Baptists* (Nashville: Sunday School Board of the Southern Baptist Convetion, 1919), 62–79.
11. W. R. White, *Baptist Distinctives* (Nashville: Sunday School Board of the Southern Baptist Convention, 1946), 30–32.
12. Henry Cook, *What Baptists Stand For* (London: Kingsgate Press, 1947), 135.
13. Robert A. Baker, *The Baptist March in History* (Nashville: Convention Press, 1958), 8.
14. Jack Hoad, *The Baptist: An Historical and Theological Study of the Baptist Identity* (London: Grace Publications Trust, 1986), 238–44.
15. Walter Rauschenbusch, *Why I Am a Baptist* (Philadelphia: Baptist Leader, 1958), in *Rochester Baptist Monthly* 20 (1905–06), 7–8.
16. John D. Freeman, "The Place of Baptists in the Christian Church," in *Baptist World Congress, London, July 11–19, 1905. Authorised Record of Proceedings* (London: Baptist Union Publication Department, 1905), 27–28.

17. E. Y. Mullins, *The Axioms of Religion: A New Interpretation of the Baptist Faith* (Philadelphia: Griffith & Rowland, 1908), 166.
18. Ibid., 238–45.
19. Philip Jones, *A Restatement of Baptist Principles* (Philadelphia: Griffith & Rowland Press, 1909), 52.
20. H. Wheeler Robinson, *Baptist Principles* 4th ed. (London: Kingsgate Press, 1966), 13.
21. H. Wheeler Robinson, *The Life and Faith of the Baptists,* (London: Kingsgate Press, 1966), 80.
22. James Kirtley, *The Baptist Distinctive and Objective* (Philadelphia: Judson Press, 1926), 11.
23. James Henry Rushbrooke, *Protestant of the Protestants: The Baptist Churches, Their Progress, and Their Spiritual Principle* (London: Kingsgate Press, 1926), 81–82.
24. James D. Mosteller, "Basic Baptist Principles and the Contemporary Scene," *Southwestern Journal of Theology* 6 (April 1964): 67–68.
25. Wayne E. Ward, "Who Is a Baptist? Believer's Baptism," *Western Recorder* (25 April 1970): 2.
26. Paul Beasley-Murray, *Radical Believers: The Baptist Way of Being the Church* (London: Baptist Union of Great Britain, 1992), 9–11.

CHAPTER 7, A DISTINCTIVE POLITY

1. John Quincy Adams, *Baptists the Only Thorough Religious Reformers,* rev. ed. (New York: Sheldon & Co., 1876), 147–48.
2. Ibid., 122.
3. Ibid., 121–23.
4. John A. Broadus, *The Duty of Baptists to Teach Their Distinctive Views* (Philadelphia: American Baptist Publication Society, 1881), 10.
5. J. M. Pendleton, *Distinctive Baptist Principles* (Philadelphia: American Baptist Publication Society, 1882), 190–205.
6. T. T. Eaton, *Baptist Why and Why Not* (Nashville: Sunday School Board of the Southern Baptist Convention, 1900), 118, 281.
7. J. B. Moody, *The Distinguishing Doctrines of Baptists* (Nashville: Folk & Browder, 1901), 182–98.
8. B. H. Carroll, *Baptists and Their Doctrines; Sermons on*

Distinctive Baptist Principles, comp. by J. B. Cranfill (Chicago: F. H. Revell Co., 1913), 32–33.

9. George W. McDaniel, *The People Called Baptists* (Nashville: Sunday School Board of the Southern Baptist Convetion, 1919), 55–61.

10. Frederick L. Anderson, *Historic Baptist Principles* (Buffalo, N.Y.: American Baptist Historical Society, 1920), 19.

11. W. R. White, *Baptist Distinctives* (Nashville: Sunday School Board of the Southern Baptist Convention, 1946), 42.

12. P. Lovene, *Distinctive Baptist Principles,* 2nd ed. rev. (Chicago: Baptist Conference Press, 1950), 12–13.

13. William H. Rone, *The Baptist Faith and Roman Catholicism,* rev. ed. (Kingsport, Tenn.: Kingsport Press, 1952), 116.

14. Henry Cook, *What Baptists Stand For* (London: Kingsgate Press, 1947), 78–79.

15. Jack Hoad, *The Baptist: An Historical and Theological Study of the Baptist Identity* (London: Grace Publications Trust, 1986), 30.

16. Walter Rauschenbusch, *Why I Am a Baptist* (Philadelphia: Baptist Leader, 1958), in *Rochester Baptist Monthly* 20 (1905–06), 5–6.

17. Ibid., 6.

18. John D. Freeman, "The Place of Baptists in the Christian Church," in *Baptist World Congress, London, July 11–19, 1905. Authorised Record of Proceedings* (London: Baptist Union Publication Department, 1905), 23.

19. E. Y. Mullins, *The Axioms of Religion: A New Interpretation of the Baptist Faith* (Philadelphia: Griffith & Rowland, 1908), 55–56.

20. Philip Jones, *A Restatement of Baptist Principles* (Philadelphia: Griffith & Rowland Press, 1909), 44.

21. H. Wheeler Robinson, *The Life and Faith of the Baptists* (London: Kingsgate Press, 1966), 86–104.

22. James Kirtley, *The Baptist Distinctive and Objective* (Philadelphia: Judson Press, 1926), 16–17.

23. James Henry Rushbrooke, *Protestant of the Protestants: The Baptist Churches, Their Progress, and Their Spiritual Principle* (London: Kingsgate Press, 1926), 78.

24. James D. Mosteller, "Basic Baptist Principles and the Contemporary Scene," in *Southwestern Journal of Theology* 6 (April 1964): 69–71.

25. Wayne E. Ward, "Who Is a Baptist? Believer's Church," *Western Recorder* (2 May 1970): 2.

26. Justice C. Anderson, "Old Baptist Principles Reset," *Southwestern Journal of Theology* 31 (Spring 1989): 9.

27. Paul Beasley-Murray, *Radical Believers: The Baptist Way of Being the Church* (London: Baptist Union of Great Britain, 1992), 58–66.

CHAPTER 8, A DISTINCTIVE COMPETENCY

1. John Quincy Adams, *Baptists the Only Thorough Religious Reformers*, rev. ed. (New York: Sheldon & Co., 1876), 90–97.

2. J. M. Pendleton, *Distinctive Baptist Principles* (Philadelphia: American Baptist Publication Society, 1882), 185.

3. T. T. Eaton, *The Faith of Baptists* (Louisville: Baptist Book Concern, 1903), 17.

4. Eaton, *Baptist Why and Why Not* (Nashville: Sunday School Board of the Southern Baptist Convention, 1900), 276–78.

5. Benjamin O. True, *Baptist Principles Reset*, 232–41.

6. B. H. Carroll, *Baptists and Their Doctrines; Sermons on Distinctive Baptist Principles*, comp. by J. B. Cranfill (Chicago: F. H. Revell Co., 1913), 15–18.

7. W. R. White, *Baptist Distinctives* (Nashville: Sunday School Board of the Southern Baptist Convention, 1946), 12.

8. P. Lovene, *Distinctive Baptist Principles*, 2nd ed. rev. (Chicago: Baptist Conference Press, 1950), 12–13.

9. William H. Rone, *The Baptist Faith and Roman Catholicism*, rev. ed. (Kingsport, Tenn.: Kingsport Press, 1952), 156.

10. Henry Cook, *What Baptists Stand For* (London: Kingsgate Press, 1947), 169–74.

11. Jack Hoad, *The Baptist: An Historical and Theological Study of the Baptist Identity* (London: Grace Publications Trust, 1986), 231.

12. Walter Rauschenbusch, *Why I Am a Baptist* (Philadelphia: Baptist Leader, 1958), in *Rochester Baptist Monthly* 20 (1905–06), 3.

13. John D. Freeman, "The Place of Baptists in the Christian Church," in *Baptist World Congress, London, July 11–19, 1905. Authorised Record of Proceedings* (London: Baptist Union Publication Department, 1905), 23–24.

14. E. Y. Mullins, *The Axioms of Religion: A New Interpretation of the Baptist Faith* (Philadelphia: Griffith & Rowland, 1908), 44, 53–58.

15. Philip Jones, *A Restatement of Baptist Principles* (Philadelphia: Griffith & Rowland Press, 1909), 16–17.

16. Ibid., 18.
17. H. Wheeler Robinson, *Life and Faith of the Baptists* (London: Kingsgate Press, 1966), 11–12.
18. James Kirtley, *The Baptist Distinctive and Objective* (Philadelphia: Judson Press, 1926), 7–8.
19. James Henry Rushbrooke, *Protestant of the Protestants: The Baptist Churches, Their Progress, and Their Spiritual Principle* (London: Kingsgate Press, 1926), 75–78.
20. James D. Mosteller, "Basic Baptist Principles and the Contemporary Scene," *Southwestern Journal of Theology* 6 (April 1964): 73.
21. Wayne E. Ward, "Who Is a Baptist? Religious Liberty," *Western Recorder* 9 (May 1970), 2.
22. Paul Beasley-Murray, *Radical Believers: The Baptist Way of Being the Church*, (London: Baptist Union of Great Britain, 1992), 60–61.

CHAPTER 9, A DISTINCTIVE FREEDOM

1. J. B. Jeter, *Baptist Principles Reset, Consisting of a Series of Articles on Distinctive Baptist Principles*, 3rd ed. (Richmond, Va.: Religious Herald, 1902), 122.
2. John Quincy Adams, *Baptists the Only Thorough Religious Reformers*, rev. ed. (New York: Sheldon & Co., 1876), 97.
3. John A. Broadus, *The Duty of Baptists to Teach Their Distinctive Views* (Philadelphia: American Baptist Publication Society, 1881), 10.
4. J. M. Pendleton, *Distinctive Baptist Principles* (Philadelphia: American Baptist Publication Society, 1882), 185–86.
5. T. T. Eaton, *Baptist Why and Why Not* (Nashville: Sunday School Board of the Southern Baptist Convention, 1900), 273–75.
6. B. H. Carroll, *Baptists and Their Doctrines; Sermons on Distinctive Baptist Principles*, comp. by J. B. Cranfill (Chicago: F. H. Revell Co., 1913), 23–24.
7. W. R. White, *Baptist Distinctives* (Nashville: Sunday School Board of the Southern Baptist Convention, 1946), 13.
8. P. Lovene, *Distinctive Baptist Principles*, 2nd ed. rev. (Chicago: Baptist Conference Press, 1950), 12–13.
9. William H. Rone, *The Baptist Faith and Roman Catholicism*, rev. ed. (Kingsport, Tenn.: Kingsport Press, 1952), 172–73.
10. Henry Cook, *What Baptists Stand For* (London: Kingsgate Press, 1947), 167.

11. Walter Rauschenbusch, *Why I Am a Baptist* (Philadelphia: Baptist Leader, 1958), in *Rochester Baptist Monthly* 20 (1905–06), 6.

12. John D. Freeman, "The Place of Baptists in the Christian Church," in *Baptist World Congress, London, July 11–19, 1905. Authorised Record of Proceedings* (London: Baptist Union Publication Department, 1905), 24–26.

13. E. Y. Mullins, *The Axioms of Religion: A New Interpretation of the Baptist Faith* (Philadelphia: Griffith & Rowland, 1908), 54–55.

14. Philip Jones, *A Restatement of Baptist Principles* (Philadelphia: Griffith & Rowland Press, 1909), 73–78.

15. George Edwin Horr, *The Baptist Heritage* (Philadelphia: Judson Press, 1923), 94–95.

16. H. Wheeler Robinson, *The Life and Faith of Baptists* (London: Kingsgate Press, 1966), 148, 166–67.

17. James Kirtley, *The Baptist Distinctive and Objective* (Philadelphia: Judson Press, 1926), 20–21.

18. James D. Mosteller, "Basic Baptist Principles and the Contemporary Scene," *Southwestern Journal of Theology* 6 (April 1964): 71–75.

19. Wayne E. Ward, "Who Is a Baptist? Religious Liberty," *Western Recorder,* 9 (May 1970): 2.

20. Norman Cavendar, "Freedom for the Church in a Free State," in *Being Baptist Means Freedom,* ed. Alan Neely (Charlotte, N.C.: Southern Baptist Alliance, 1988), 85–89.

CONCLUSION: DISTINCTIVELY BAPTIST

1. Fisher Humphreys, *The Way We Were: How Southern Baptist Theology Has Changed and What It Means to Us All* (New York: MacCracken Press, 1994), 33–54.

2. *Baptist Why and Why Not* (Nashville: Sunday School Board of the Southern Baptist Convention, 1900), 19–20.

3. Millard J. Erickson, *The New Evangelical Theology* (London: Marshall, Morgan, and Scott, 1969), 30–45.

Selected Bibliography

....

PRIMARY SOURCES

BOOKS

Adams, John Quincy. *Baptists the Only Thorough Religious Reformers.*
 Rev. ed. New York: Sheldon & Co., 1876.

Adams, Robert John. *Baptist Churches Compared with Those of Other
 Denominations.* n.p., 1873.

Adkins, Frank. *Disciples and Baptists. Their Resemblances and
 Differences in Belief and Practice.* Philadelphia: American Baptist
 Publication Soceity, 1896.

Adkins, Frank. *Distinctions between Campbellites and Baptists.*
 Cincinnati: G. W. Lasher, n.d.

Anderson, Frederick Lincoln. *Historic Baptist Principles.* Buffalo, N.Y.:
 American Baptist Historical Society, 1920.

*An Answer to the Question, What Are the Distinguishing Tenets of the
 Baptists?* n.p., n.d.

Anderson, Galusha. *Distinctive Principles of the Baptists. A Resume.*
 Philadelphia: American Baptist Publication Society, n.d.

Armitage, Thomas. "Baptist Faith and Practice." *Baptist Doctrines,* ed.
 Charles A. Jenkens. St. Louis: Chancy R. Barns, 1881.

Armstrong, J. Murray. *Baptist Principles Relevant for the Space Age?* St.
 John, N.B.: Union Jubilee Committee, 1966–69.

Baker, Joseph S. *The Sects Versus the Baptists: An Appeal in Behalf of the Defendants from the Decisions of Popes, Presbyters, and Prelatic Councils, to an Enlightened Public. By an Advocate of Equity.* Jacksonville, Fla.: C. Drew's Book and Job Printing Office, 1858.

Baker, Robert Andrew. *The Baptist March in History.* Nashville: Convention Press, 1958.

Baptist Jubilee Advance Committee. *Baptist Distinctives and Disagreements and Differences of Emphasis among Baptists.* Valley Forge, Pa.: Judson Press for the Baptist Jubilee Advance Committee, 1964.

Baptist Why and Why Not. Nashville: Sunday School Board, Southern Baptist Convention, 1900.

Batey, J. "Distinctive Principles." *The English Baptists, Who They Are, and What They Have Done,* ed. John Clifford. London: E. Marlborough, 1881.

Beasley-Murray, Paul. *Radical Believers: The Baptist Way of Being the Church.* London: Baptist Union of Great Britain, 1992.

Boggs, William Bambrick. *The Baptists: Who Are They? and What Do They Believe?* 4th ed. Philadelphia: American Baptist Publication Society, 1898.

Boone, William Cooke. *What We Believe.* Nashville: Sunday School Board of the Southern Baptist Convention, 1936.

Bow, Jonathan Gaines. *What Baptists Believe and Why They Believe It.* Nashville: Sunday School Board of the Southern Baptist Convention, 1906.

Brayton, Durlin Lee. *Who Are the Baptists? Their Distinctive Principles and Practice.* n.p., 1891.

Broadus, John Albert. *The Duty of Baptists to Teach Their Distinctive Views.* Philadelphia: American Baptist Publication Society, 1881.

Burrows, John Lansing. *What Baptists Believe.* Baltimore: H. M. Wharton & Co., 1887.

Buttrick, Wallace. *Distinctive Views of Baptists.* n.p., n.d.

Carroll, Benajah Harvey. *Baptists and Their Doctrines; Sermons on Distinctive Baptist Principles.* Comp. J. B. Cranfill. Chicago: F. H. Revell Co., 1913.

Carter, Joseph E. *Distinctive Baptist Principles.* Raleigh, N.C.: Edwards, Broughton, and Co., 1883.

Cavendar, Norman. "Freedom for the Church in a Free State." In *Being Baptist Means Freedom,* ed. Alan Neely. Charlotte, N.C.: Southern Baptist Alliance, 1988.

Cook, Henry. *What Baptists Stand For.* London: Kingsgate Press, 1947.

Curtis, Thomas F. *The Progress of Baptist Principles.* Philadelphia: American Baptist Publication Society, 1855.

Cutting, Sewall Sylvester. *The Position and Peculiarities of Baptists, Defined and Illustrated.* Boston: Gould, Kendall and Lincoln, 1842.

Davies, James Philip. *The Position of the Baptists in Comparison with Other Denominations.* Morriston, Wales: n.p., 1894.

Davis, Gustavus Fellows. "A Vindication of the Peculiar Sentiments of the Baptist Denomination." In A. L. Davis, *Memoir of Rev. G. F. Davis.* n.p., n.d.

Dodd, Monroe Elmon. *A Comparison and Contrast.* Nashville: Sunday School Board of the Southern Baptist Convention, n.d.

Eaton, Thomas Treadwell. *The Faith of the Baptists.* Louisville: Baptist Book Concern, 1903.

Fant, Clyde. "Reaching Out with the Bible." In *Proclaiming the Baptist Vision: The Bible,* ed. Walter B. Shurden. Macon, Ga.: Smyth and Helwys, 1994.

Fickett, Harold Lord, Sr. *Baptist Beliefs. A Series of Seven Studies in Distinctive Doctrines.* n.p., 1943.

Forrester, E. J. *The Baptist Position as to the Bible, the Church, and the Ordinances.* Baltimore: R. H. Woodward, 1893.

Freeman, John D. "The Place of Baptists in the Christian Church." In *Baptist World Congress. London, July 11–19, 1905. Authorised Record of Proceedings.* London: Baptist Union Publication Department, 1905.

Gambrell, James Burton and others. *Baptist Principles Reset, Consisting of a Series of Articles on Distinctive Baptist Principles.* 3rd ed. Richmond, Va.: Religious Herald, 1902.

Gaustad, Edwin S. "Toward a Baptist Identity in the Twenty-first Century." In *Discovering Our Baptist Heritage,* ed. William H. Brackney, Valley Forge, Pa.: The American Baptist Historical Society, 1985.

Gezork, Herbert. "Our Baptist Faith in the World To-Day." In *Baptist World Alliance Golden Jubilee Congress, London, 1955.* London: Kingsgate Press, 1955.

Grantham, Thomas. *Presumption No Proof, or, Mr. Petto's Arguments for Infant Baptism, Considered and Answered.* London: n.p., 1687.

Greer, E. Eugene, Jr., ed. *Baptists: History, Distinctives, and Relationships.* Dallas: Baptist General Convention of Texas, 1996.

Griffith, Earle G. *Baptists: Their History, Principles, and Polity.* New York: Interstate Evangelistic Association, 1935.

Grove, Richard E. "The Freedom of the Local Church." In *Being Baptist Means Freedom,* Alan Neely, ed., Charlotte, N.C.: Southern Baptist Alliance, 1988.

Hanson, William. *What the Baptists Believe, and Why.* London: Elliot Stock, n.d.

Halbrooks, G. Thomas. "Why I Am a Baptist." In *Being Baptist Means Freedom,* Alan Neely, ed., Charlotte, N.C.: Southern Baptist Alliance, 1988.

Haldeman, Isaac Massey. *What the Baptist Church Stands For.* n.p., 1900.

Harley, Timothy. *Baptist Principles.* London: Baptist Tract Depository, 1882.

Haynes, D. C. *The Baptist Denomination: Its History, Doctrines, and Ordinances.* New York: Sheldon, Blakeman, & Co., 1856.

Hays, Brooks and John E. Steely. *The Baptist Way of Life.* Englewood Cliffs, N.J.: Prentice-Hall, Inc., 1963.

Hiscox, Edward Thurston. *New Directory for Baptist Churches.* Philadelphia: American Baptist Publication Society, 1894.

Hoad, Jack. *The Baptists: An Historical and Theological Study of the Baptist Identity.* London: Grace Publications Trust, 1986.

Horr, George Edwin. *The Baptist Heritage.* Philadelphia: Judson Press, 1923.

Hovey, Alvah. *Restatement of Denominational Principles.* Philadelphia: American Baptist Publication Society, 1892.

Hovey, Alvah and others. *Baptist Principles Reset, Consisting of a Series of Articles on Distinctive Baptist Principles.* 3rd ed. Richmond, Va.: Religious Herald, 1902.

Hudson, Winthrop Still. *Baptist Convictions.* Valley Forge, Pa.: Judson Press, 1963.

Humphreys, Fisher. *The Way We Were: How Southern Baptist Theology Has Changed and What It Means to Us All.* New York: McCracken Press, 1994.

Jeter, Jeremiah Bell and others. *Baptist Principles Reset, Consisting of a Series of Articles on Distinctive Baptist Principles.* 3rd ed. Richmond, Va.: Religious Herald, 1902.

Jones, Philip L. *A Restatement of Baptist Principles.* Philadelphia: Griffith & Rowland Press, 1909.

Kerfoot, Franklin Howard. *Distinctive Doctrines of the Baptists.* Louisville: Baptist Argus, 1898.

Kilpatrick, James H. *The Baptists: Their First Appearance and Something of Their History; Their Principles, Doctrines, and Obligations.* Atlanta: Georgia Baptist Association, 1911.

Kirtley, James S. *The Baptist Distinctive and Objective.* Philadelphia: Judson Press, 1926.

Lovene, P. *Distinctive Baptist Principles.* 2nd ed. rev. Chicago: Baptist Conference Press, 1950.

MacArthur, Robert Stuart. *The Baptists: Their Principle, Their Progress, Their Prospect.* Philadelphia: American Baptist Publication Society, 1911.

Manley, Ken. *Who Are the Baptists?* Hawthorne, Victoria: Clifford Press, 1982.

Maring, Norman H. and Winthrop Still Hudson. *A Baptist Manual of Polity and Practice.* Chicago: Judson Press, 1963.

McDaniel, George White. *The People Called Baptists*. Nashville: Sunday School Board of the Southern Baptist Convention, 1919.

McNutt, William Roy. *Polity and Practice in Baptist Churches*. Philadelphia: Judson Press, 1935.

Moody, Joseph Burnley. *The Distinguishing Doctrines of Baptists*. Nashville: Folk & Browder, 1901.

Mosher, Roswell Curtis. *The Distinctive Principle of Baptists*. n.p., n.d.

Mullins, Edgar Young. *The Axioms of Religion: A New Interpretation of the Baptist Faith*. Philadelphia: Griffith & Rowland, 1908.

Neely, Alan, ed. *Being Baptist Means Freedom*. Charlotte, N.C.: Southern Baptist Alliance, 1988.

Nowlin, William Dudley. *What Baptists Stand For*. Louisville: Baptist Book Concern, 1918.

Odle, Joe T. *Why I Am a Baptist*. Nashville: Broadman Press, 1972.

Pendleton, James Madison. *Distinctive Baptist Principles*. Philadelphia: American Baptist Publication Society, 1882.

_____. *Three Reasons Why I Am a Baptist; With a Fourth Reason Added on Communion*. 13th ed. Nashville: Graves, Marks, and Rutland, 1856.

Pollard, John. *Baptist Doctrines: The Practical Effect They Ought to Have on Those Professing Them; or Baptists Called by Their Principles to Be the Best People in the World*. Richmond, Va.: Pitt & Dickinson, 1901.

Porter, John William. *Differences between Baptists and Campbellites*. Lexington, Ky.: Mr. J. W. Porter, 1938.

Ramay, Marion Edgar. *Basic Baptist Principles*. Shawnee, Okla.: Oklahoma Baptist University Press, 1951.

_____. *Plain Statements on Baptist Faith and Practice*. Oklahoma City: Messenger Press, 1957.

Robinson, Henry Wheeler. *Baptist Principles*. 4th ed. London: Kingsgate Press, 1966.

_____. *The Life and Faith of the Baptists*. London: Kingsgate Press, 1946.

Robertson, Benjamin Perry. *Distinctive Baptist Principles*. Greenville, S.C.: Keys and Thomas, n.d.

Rone, William Holmes. *The Baptist Faith and Roman Catholicism*. Rev. ed. Kingsport, Tenn.: Kingsport Press, 1952.

Runquist, Felix. *Baptist Distinctives*. Minneapolis: Central C. Baptist Tract Society, n.d.

Rushbrooke, James Henry. *Protestant of the Protestants: The Baptist Churches, Their Progress, and Their Spiritual Principle*. London: Kingsgate Press, 1926.

Ryland, John. *A Candid Statement of the Reasons Which Induce the Baptists to Differ in Opinion and Practice from So Many of Their Christian Brethren*. Philadelphia: Anderson and Meehan, 1820.

Shelley, Bruce. *What Baptists Believe.* Wheaton, Ill: C. B. Press, 1973.

Shurden, Walter B., ed. *The Baptist Identity: Four Fragile Freedoms.* Macon, Ga.: Smyth & Helwys, 1993.

Sherman, Cecil E. "Freedom of the Individual to Interpret the Bible." In *Being Baptist Means Freedom,* ed. Alan Neely. Charlotte, N.C.: Southern Baptist Alliance, 1988.

Skevington, S. F. *The Distinctive Principles of the Baptists.* Printed for private distribution, 1914.

Sloan, William Alva. *Baptist Distinctives and the Origin of Different Denominations.* n.p., 1930.

Sproles, Henry Franklin. *Differences between Baptists and Other Denominations.* Philadelphia: American Baptist Publication Society, n.d.

Staton, Cecil. *Why I Am a Baptist: Reflections on Being Baptist in the 21st Century.* Macon, Ga.: Smyth & Helwys, 1999.

Stedman, G. C. *Debate on Some of the Distinctive Differences between the Reformers and Baptists.* Louisville: n.p., 1858.

Theophilus [pseud.] *An Appeal to Baptists in Their Necessity and Importance of the Maintenance of Their Denominational Principles as Essential to the Establishment of Their Kingdom of God upon Earth.* London: G. B. Dyer, 1841.

True, Benjamin O. and others. *Baptist Principles Reset, Consisting of a Series of Articles on Distinctive Baptist Principles.* 3rd ed. Richmond, Va.: Religious Herald, 1902.

Turner, John Clyde. *Our Baptist Heritage.* Nashville: Sunday School Board of the Southern Baptist Convention, 1945.

Walthall, J. S. *The Distinctive Features of the Baptists.* Raleigh, N.C.: Strother and Marcom, 1861.

Whitby, F. F. *Baptist Principles.* London: Kingsgate Press, n.d.

White, William Richardson. *Baptist Distinctives.* Nashville: Sunday School Board of the Southern Baptist Convention, 1946.

Whitley, William Thomas. *The Witness of History to Baptist Principles.* Rev. ed. London: Kingsgate Press, 1914.

JOURNAL ARTICLES

Anderson, Justice C. "Old Baptist Principles Reset." *Southwestern Journal of Theology* 31 (Spring 1989): 5–12.

Davies, Emlyn. "Our Historic Baptist Distinctives." *The Chronicle* 16 (October 1953): 191–200.

Gilkey, Charles W. "The Distinctive Baptist Witness." *The Chronicle* 8 (July 1945): 97–106.

Hine, Leland D. "Viewpoints: A Baptist Vision." *Foundations* 20 (January–March 1977): 5–11.

Mosteller, James Donovan. "Basic Baptist Principles and the

Contemporary Scene." *Southwestern Journal of Theology* 6 (April 1964): 60–81.

Ohlmann, Eric H. "The Essence of the Baptists: A Reexamination." *Perspectives in Religious Studies* 13 (Fall 1986): 83–104.

Peck, George. "The Baptist Heritage: Practice, Polity, and Promise." *Andover Newton Quarterly* 19 (March 1979): 215–22.

PERIODICALS

Rauschenbusch, Walter. *Why I Am a Baptist.* Philadelphia: Baptist Leader, 1958. In *Rochester Baptist Monthly* 20 (1905–06), 2–3.

Ward, Wayne E. "What Is a Baptist? Personal Religious Freedom." *Western Recorder,* 4 April 1970.

_____. "Who Is a Baptist? The Authority of the Bible." *Western Recorder,* 11 April 1970.

_____. "Who Is a Baptist? Personal Regeneration and Faith." *Western Recorder,* 18 April 1970.

_____. "Who Is a Baptist? Believer's Baptism." *Western Recorder,* 25 April 1970.

_____. "Who Is a Baptist? Believers' Church." *Western Recorder,* 2 May 1970.

_____. "Who Is a Baptist? Religious Liberty." *Western Recorder,* 9 May 1970.

_____. "Who Is a Baptist? Separation of Church and State." *Western Recorder,* 16 May 1970.

DISSERTATIONS AND UNPUBLISHED PAPERS

Brewer, Paul D. "Our Southern Baptist Heritage." Paper presented at the Steeple and Faculty Affairs Committee of Carson-Newman College. Jefferson City, Tennessee, 1989.

Freeman, Curtis and others. "Re-Envisioning Baptist Identity: A Manifesto for Baptist Communities in North America." Unpublished paper submitted to various Baptist leaders, 1996.

Puckett, Garnett E. "Struggles of Baptists in America to Sustain Their Distinctive Principles 1639–1791." Th.D. diss., The Southern Baptist Theological Seminary, 1947.

SERMONS AND PAMPHLETS

Denison, Frederic. "Sermon on the Seven Pillars of the Baptists; Preached to the Baptist Church, Westerly, Rhode Island, June 23, 1867." Westerly, R.I.: G. B. & J. H. Utter, 1867.

Dixon, Amzi Clarence. *Points in the Baptist Position.* Philadelphia: American Baptist Publication Society, n.d.

Fuller, Richard. *Who Are the Baptists? A Short Hand Sketch of Dr.*

Fuller's Remarks at the Water, before Baptizing Dr. Cole, September 28, 1851. Baltimore: Printed at the Office of the True Union, 1851.

Furman, Richard. *A Discourse Delivered before the Baptist Church in Cheraw, S.C., August 23, 1840: In Vindication of the Doctrine and Practice of the Baptist Denomination.* Cheraw, S.C.: Wm. Potter, 1840.

Garrett, James Leo, Jr. "Baptist 'Distinctives': Endangered Species." Sermon at Southwestern Baptist Theological Seminary in Fort Worth, Texas, 4 September 1991.

McDaniel, George White. "Distinctive Features of the Baptists." Richmond, Va.: n.p., 1906.

Patterson, Paige, ed. *We Believe: Sermons on Baptist Doctrine.* Dallas: Criswell Publications, 1977.

Stowell, Austin H. "The Communion Question, Embracing the Distinctive Features of the Baptist Denomination: A Doctrinal Sermon." Fall River, Mass.: Henry Pratt, 1860.

Thomas, Charles Alexander Gard. *The Duty of Baptists to Teach Their Distinctive Principles . . . Delivered Jan. 28, 1898.* Raleigh, N.C.: Biblical Recorder Print, n.d.

Underhill, Edward Bean. *The Distinctive Features of the Baptist Denomination. A Discourse Delivered at the Opening of the Thirty-ninth Annual Session of the Baptist Union of Great Britain and Ireland, April 25th, 1851.* London: Houlston and Stonemen, 1851.

Walthall, J. S. "The Distinctive Features of the Baptists: A Sermon Delivered before the Union Association at Its Session, Oct. 9–12, 1860." Raleigh, N.C.: Strother & Marcom, 1861.

SECONDARY SOURCES

BOOKS

Barr, James. *The Semantics of Biblical Language.* New York: Oxford University Press, 1961.

Basden, Paul A. "Predestination." In *Has Our Theology Changed? Southern Baptist Theology Since 1845,* ed. Paul A. Basden. Nashville: Broadman & Holman, 1994.

Berkhof, Louis. *The History of Christian Doctrines.* Grand Rapids: Baker Book House, 1937.

Bloom, Harold. *The American Religion: The Emergence of the Post-Christian Nation.* New York: Simon and Schuster, 1992.

Bush, L. Russ and Thomas J. Nettles. *Baptists and the Bible.* Chicago: Moody Press, 1980.

Childs, Brevard. *Biblical Theology in Crisis.* Philadelphia: Westminster Press, 1970.

Cook, Martin. *The Open Circle*. Minneapolis: Fortress Press, 1991.

Draughon, Walter D., III. "Atonement." In *Has Our Theology Changed? Southern Baptist Theology Since 1845*, ed. Paul A. Basden. Nashville: Broadman & Holman, 1994.

Ellis, William E. *"A Man of Books and a Man of the People": E. Y. Mullins and the Crisis of Moderate Southern Baptist Leadership.* Macon, Ga.: Mercer University Press, 1985.

Erickson, Millard J. *Christian Theology*. Grand Rapids: Baker Book House, 1985.

———. *The New Evangelical Theology*. London: Marshall, Morgan, and Scott, 1969.

Garrett, James Leo., Jr. *Systematic Theology*. Vol. 1. Grand Rapids: Wm. B. Eerdmans, 1990.

George, Timothy. *Baptist Confessions, Covenants, and Catechisms*. Nashville: Broadman & Holman, 1996.

Gilmore, A., ed. *The Pattern of the Church: A Baptist View*. London: Lutterworth Press, 1963.

Gonzavlez, Justo L. *A History of Christian Thought*. 3 vols. Rev. ed. Nashville: Abingdon Press, 1991.

Graves, J. R. *Old Landmarkism: What Is It?* 2nd ed. Memphis: Baptist Book House, 1881.

Grudem, Wayne. *Systematic Theology: An Introduction to Biblical Doctrine*. Grand Rapids: Zondervan Publishing, 1994.

Harnack, Adolf von. *History of Dogma*. 7 vols. London: Williams & Norgate, 1896-99.

Hobbs, Herschel H. *The Axioms of Religion*. Rev. ed. Nashville: Broadman Press, 1978.

Hudson, Winthrop Still, ed. *Baptist Concepts of the Church*. Chicago: Judson Press, 1959.

McBeth, H. Leon. *English Baptist Literature on Religious Liberty to 1689*. New York: Arno Press, 1980.

McCall, Duke K., ed. *What Is the Church?* Nashville: Broadman Press, 1958.

McGlothlin, William J. *What Is Essential Baptist Doctrine? An Inquiry.* Louisville: C. T. Dearing Printing, n.d.

Moody, Dwight A. "The Bible." In *Has Our Theology Changed? Southern Baptist Theology Since 1845*, ed. Paul A. Basden. Nashville: Broadman & Holman, 1994.

Mullins, Edgar Young. *The Christian Religion in Its Doctrinal Expression*. Boston: Judson Press, 1917.

———. *Freedom and Authority in Religion*. Philadelphia: Griffith & Rowland Press, 1913.

———. "The Response of Jesus Christ to Modern Thought." In *Faith in the Modern World*. Nashville: Sunday School Board of the Southern Baptist Convention, 1930.

_____. *Why Is Christianity True?* Philadelphia: American Baptist
   Publication Society, 1905.
Mullins, Isla May. *Edgar Young Mullins: An Intimate Biography.*
   Nashville: Sunday School Board of the Southern Baptist Convention,
   1929.
Nettles, Thomas J. *By His Grace and for His Glory: A Historical,
   Theological, and Practical Study of the Doctrines of Grace in Baptist
   Life.* Grand Rapids: Baker Book House, 1986.
Newman, John Henry. *Essay on the Development of Christian
   Doctrine.* New York: D. Appleton & Co., n.d.
Niebuhr, H. Richard. *The Meaning of Revelation.* New York:
   Macmillan Co., 1941.
Pelikan, Jaroslav. *Historical Theology: Continuity and Change in
   Christian Doctrine.* New York: Corpus, 1971.
Schleiermacher, Friedrich. *Brief Outline on the Study of Theology.*
   Trans. Terrence N. Tice. Richmond, Va.: John Knox Press, 1966.
Tull, James. *Shapers of Baptist Thought.* Valley Forge, Pa.: Judson
   Press, 1979.
Wayland, Francis. *The Principles and Practices of Baptist Churches.*
   London: J. Heaton & Son, 1861.
Whitley, William Thomas. *A History of British Baptists.* Philadelphia: J.
   B. Lippincott, 1923.
Whitten, Mark. "Philosophy of Religion." In *Has Our Theology
   Changed? Southern Baptist Theology Since 1845,* ed. Paul A.
   Basden. Nashville: Broadman & Holman, 1994.

DICTIONARIES AND ENCYCLOPEDIAS

Baker, D. L. "Biblical Theology." *New Dictionary of Theology.*
Brown, Colin. "Philosophical Theology." *New Dictionary of Theology.*
Dobbins, Gaines S. "Mullins, Edgar Young." *Encyclopedia of Southern
   Baptists.*
Erickson, Millard J. "The Lordship of Christ." *Concise Dictionary of
   Christian Theology.*
Feinberg, Paul D. "Epistemology." *Evangelical Dictionary of Theology.*
Macquarrie, John. "Systematic Theology." *New Handbook of Christian
   Theology.*
Richardson, Alan. "Confession(s), Confessionalism." *The Westminster
   Dictionary of Christian Theology.*
Stendahl, Krister. "Biblical Theology." *The Interpreter's Dictionary
   of the Bible.*
Wilken, Robert L. "Historical Theology." *New Handbook of
   Christian Theology.*

DISSERTATIONS

Dilday, Russell Hooper. "The Apologetic Method of E. Y. Mullins."
Th.D. diss., Southwestern Baptist Theological Seminary, 1960.
Thomas, Bill Clark. "Edgar Young Mullins: A Baptist Exponent of
Theological Restatement." Ph.D., diss., Southwestern Baptist
Theological Seminary, 1963.

JOURNAL ARTICLES

Garrett, James Leo, Jr. "The History of Christian Doctrine: Retrospect
and Prospect." *Review and Expositor* 58 (Spring 1971): 245–60.
_____. "Major Emphases in Baptist Theology." *Southwestern
Journal of Theology* 37 (Summer 1995): 36–46.
_____. "Sources of Authority in Baptist Thought." *Baptist History
and Heritage* 13 (July 1978): 41–49.
McClendon, James William, Jr. "What Is a "Baptist" Theology?"
American Baptist Quarterly 1 (October 1982): 16–39.
Ramm, Bernard. "Baptist Theology." *Watchman-Examiner* 43
(November 24, 1955): 1070–73.

Name Index

....

Subject Index

....